THURLOW'S
DARTMOOR
Companion

Nature's architecture — Great Staple Tor

THURLOW'S DARTMOOR
Companion

George Thurlow

Peninsula
Press

I dedicate this book to my wife, Patricia, and to all
those kindred spirits who value the tranquillity of
wild and peaceful places.

Published by Peninsula Press Ltd
PO Box 31
Newton Abbot
Devon TQ12 5XH
Telephone (0803) 875875

© George Thurlow 1993

ISBN 1 872640 26 5

Designed by Brian Ainsworth

Printed in Hong Kong by Wing King Tong Co.Ltd.

Becka (Becky) Falls (Manaton, 761801), Dartmoor's best-known water-fall, on Becka Brook, a mile or so above its confluence with the Bovey.

Contents

Acknowledgements

It is a well-known fact that writing a book can be a lonely business, not only for the author but also for the author's companion. To my wife Patricia, then, goes an incalculable measure of gratitude for her forbearance and encouragement over a period of many years. Among those who have given me information, advice and their valuable time, special mention is due to John Weir and other members of the Dartmoor National Park staff, to the late Harry Starkey (who, as a result of my enthusiasm, may not have wanted to hear the word "gatepost" again), and to the late Ted Masson Phillips, who was not only subjected to a succession of queries but who also read the first draft.

I am particularly appreciative of the interest shown by the directors of Peninsula Press in this project, and of their friendly and painstaking collaboration.

Permission to use such material as has appeared in the *Dartmoor Magazine* has been kindly given by the magazine's editor, Miss Elizabeth Stanbrook.

One of the chimneys at
Powder Mills

Preface

Dartmoor has many faces, depending on one's point of view. It is a land of contrasts, not only in its wide range of topography (if one considers all that area included within the National Park) but in the way it has been used and abused or revered and defended. We tend to think of the high moorland as a wild and solitary place - it has been called the last wilderness in southern England - but very little of Dartmoor is untouched by the hand of man.

The age-old occupation of deriving a living from the land - and here the accent is on hill farming - forms the overriding background to all else that goes on (in recent years substantially augmented by tourism). In the distant past the moor was inhabited by a succession of prehistoric peoples (whose relics are so common here), and later there were dramatic upheavals caused by the extraction of tin and other minerals.

Human nature and human needs being what they are, man's impact on the moor fluctuates, and comparatively recently new pressures have been brought to bear, such as the demands of an ever-increasing population in terms of water-extraction, defence and afforestation. We feel at times that we are being persuaded that china clay digging for example, is only going to extend over a comparatively small area of moorland, and on the opposite side a new road is only going to encroach by a half a mile or so, and that a projected new reservoir is only going to flood a useless bog. I remember hearing, in a televised discussion, that afforestation being considered at that time would only threaten a small area - no mention being made of those areas already planted.

The sum total of all such encroachments in recent years, added to earlier (and continuing) land enclosures, is alarming, and when one considers that, with a reasonable degree of experience, one can walk across the moor in the space of a summer's day, one realises how very small it really is.

The designation of Dartmoor as a National Park gave it some measure of protection from blatant spoliation; on the other hand it has tended to increase the human impact in terms of tourism and other leisure and recreational pursuits. In contrast with those days in the not-too-distant past when it was possible to walk all day without seeing another soul, it now takes very severe conditions to keep all humanity at home, and solitude is the exception rather than the norm.

I have to admit that there are times when the moor, for me, tends to lose a little of its appeal. When the rain drives horizontally and relentlessly into one's eyes, or dripping mist obscures all but the closest features, I find no pleasure in exploration; and if I write that a feature is visible from a certain point, I mean in fair weather.

Under more favourable conditions Dartmoor is a place of beauty - a singular beauty which I would not attempt to describe (though some writers, much more able than I, with Eden Phillpotts at their head, have very nearly succeeded). There is something here more than just visual impact - the irresistible magnetism of wide open spaces, the "atmosphere", the scent of spongy turf and the muted sounds of bird and beast - and I can think of a no more agreeable environment. Beyond this, there is the appeal of walking with the additional purpose of locating specific objects of interest, many of them a result of man's activities.

Human exploitation has left a mark on Dartmoor which is more tangible than in many other areas, in no small measure because of the super-abundance of that very usable and durable commodity, the Dartmoor granite.

Paradoxically, some of us tend to revere the relics of the spoliation of yesteryear, whilst vigorously resisting current change. Be that as it may, the quest for many of the signs of man's influence on the face of the moor takes us to places once bustling with activity, but now quiet, wild and beautiful, where we can feel above materialism, and at peace with ourselves and with that remote world outside.

Not long after I began exploring the moor I felt I ought to try to combine some of my leisure interests into a cohesive project. One of the results is a collection of drawings, most of them made from my own photographs. As the latter were taken over a period of many years, some of the subjects are no longer as they used to be. On Dartmoor changes tend to occur at an alarming rate, even to some of the seemingly most intransient things; the disappearance of the Nutcracker on the slope of Rippon Tor is but one example (see page 39). My drawings of such features have been retained.

My choice of subject matter reflects my own particular range of interests in Dartmoor, and there are many aspects of the Dartmoor scene I have not touched upon. These are dealt with in their proper place, and I am fully aware that I merely scratched the surface of this fascinating subject. But I hope that the features I have included will serve as a reminder of some of the things which make Dartmoor unique, and perhaps will bring about many enjoyable days seeking them out.

There is one view of Dartmoor (or rather a multiplicity of views) which should be specially mentioned - Dartmoor as seen from the air. Aerial photographs, as related to this region, are particularly relevant in revealing the existence of early field boundaries, habitation sites and other patterns of disturbance. Such views are becoming increasingly available, and the wealth of information contained in them (see Greeves, 1985) promises to open up new horizons for the future.

George Thurlow
Ideford, Devon

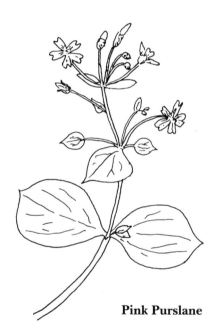

Pink Purslane

Notes

1. In presenting a factual statement of my perception of the Dartmoor scene, one of my intentions was to avoid controversial issues. However some of what I have written is flavoured by opinion.

2. My treatment of each of the categories is variable, ranging from attempts to include all known examples of features of a similar type, if space permits, to a general review where examples are too numerous for individual mention.

3. It will be seen that there is some variation in the spelling of place-names. In such a region, low in resident population and, until recent times, in recorded topography, it is not necessarily important to pursue the question of "correct" spellings, or to be consistent, so long as meanings are clear and do not infer misleading derivations - in fact, in order to indicate alternative spellings, I have been deliberately inconsistent.

4. A National Grid reference indicates the square in which a feature is situated. The prefix SX is not used, as it applies to the whole of Dartmoor. The 10km square in which a feature is to be found is indicated by the first digit of each triplet in a six-figure reference (e.g. Nun's Cross, at 601699, is in square SX66), and by the first digit of each pair in a four-figure reference.

5. Whilst acknowledging the shift towards metrication I do not feel it illogical to retain the imperial system of measurement in a book related mainly to the past. Milestones bear little relationship to kilometres, and it seems reasonable to record, for example, that the cider vat at Longstone measures 4ft x 3ft x 2ft, and that the mysterious octagonal artefact in Widecombe church is 2ft across the flats (as, incidentally, are the bases of the columns and the font).

6. Mention of Crossing or Worth in the text relates to the major works under their names in the Bibliography - Crossing's _Guide_ and Worth's _Dartmoor_. References to other titles are normally indicated by the name of the author and the date.

7. Apart from the very important subject of **access restrictions** mentioned below, the only comment I would make on the fundamentals of Dartmoor exploration relates to the Country Code. I have always been a little doubtful about the inflexibility of the clause regarding the shutting of gates, and wondered whether a farmer might *want* to leave a gate open. I once put this to the test by shutting an open gate, and on my return found it tied open.

ABBREVIATIONS

DAS	Devon Archaeological Society
DM	*Dartmoor Magazine*
DNPA	Dartmoor National Park Authority
DPA	Dartmoor Preservation Association
ProcDAS	Proceedings of the Devon Archaeological Society
TDA	Transactions of the Devonshire Association

The whole of the land on Dartmoor is privately owned, and reference on any page of this book to any location which is not indisputably a public place (even though it may appear to be so), or to any feature which is in such a place, does not infer that there is a right of access to that location or feature.

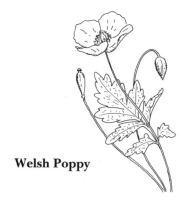

Welsh Poppy

Part I

THE LIE OF THE LAND

Introduction

Dartmoor forms part of the granite backbone of the south-west peninsula, and extends over much of South Devon. The lush farmlands which surround it overlie a fascinating variety of geological formations, seen to great effect along the popular coastal strip to the south and east, where the dominant features are cliffs of red sandstone, shales, slate and limestone.

The main routes from the Midlands and the east diverge at Exeter, to pass the moor on the north and south, going towards Cornwall via Okehampton or Plymouth respectively; these two centres of population are connected by a road which skirts the moor's western edge by way of Tavistock. Most of the towns and villages lie around the perimeter and in the north-east sector where there is an extensive network of minor roads and lanes.

The limits of the moor are variable according to one's own personal viewpoint. Over very many years increasing areas of moorland have been enclosed, and have, in part, become akin to the countryside around its fringe (the "in-country").

As a relatively wild area, and one of outstanding beauty, Dartmoor was in 1951 designated a National Park. When established it took in an area of 365 square miles, but this included much of the enclosed country outside the moorland proper, particularly in the north-east sector around Moretonhampstead. It excluded, however, some of the open moorland being increasingly exploited industrially in the south-west, in the vicinity of Lee Moor.

Be that as it may, the countryside contained within the National Park boundary is a convenient study area, give or take a little here or there.

Dartmoor can be thought of as a hilly plateau, at two sliqhtly different average levels, with a central depression or "basin" separating these two main areas, the northern and southern moors. This natural division, with which the Dart and its tributaries claim a relevant relationship, is reinforced by the presence of the trans-moor highways which intersect at Two Bridges. Most of the moor is above 1000ft, with an average elevation of about 1200; it rises to just over 2000ft at the hiqhest points, Yes Tor and High Willhayes.

Because the granite is largely decomposed, the typical scene on the high moors is of rounded hills and shallow valleys. The effect of heat on the overlying sedimentary rocks during the formation of the granite caused them to change in character, and this altered rock has eroded from the main moorland area. There is, however, a residual rim around the margin of the moor (the metamorphic aureole). Where the rivers approach this band there are deep gorges - the rocks of the valley sides having resisted such opening nut as has occurred at higher levels. (Lydford Gorge, a spectacular fissure within the north-west boundary of the National Park, is a different case, as it lies in Upper Devonian slate, beyond the metamorphic aureole) .

On the moor the climate tends towards the inclement, the atmosphere is humid, and the soil is impoverished. These factors, combined with a unique pattern of industry, have contributed to the existence of this very special environment.

The Forest and parishes

The whole of Devon was once a "forest", that is to say the sovereign's hunting preserve, no doubt because it was at that time one of the remaining areas still well covered by trees. With the exception of Dartmoor and Exmoor the county was disafforested in 1204 (thus freeing its inhabitants from the burden of the harsh Forest laws).

Soon afterwards the Forest of Dartmoor, together with the manor of Lydford and Lydford Castle, was passed to the Duchy of Cornwall, becoming, as it still is, technically, a "chase".

The Forest, now virtually devoid of native trees, consists of a large central area of Dartmoor, 56000 acres in extent, included entirely within the parish of Lydford until 1987. Its bounds have been set out at various times, notably in 1240 when a perambulation was undertaken by twelve knights. There have been differences of opinion between the Duchy and Commoners on certain details of the boundary, but these have been finally resolved.

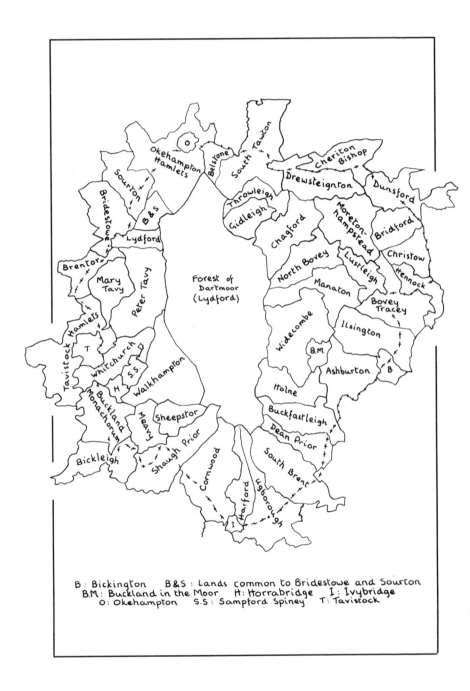

B : Bickington   B&S : Lands common to Bridestowe and Sourton
B.M. : Buckland in the Moor   H : Horrabridge   I : Ivybridge
O : Okehampton   S.S : Sampford Spiney   T : Tavistock

To facilitate leasing and management the Forest is divided into four Quarters (North, South, East and West).

The parishes range in size from immense areas such as Widecombe and Walkhampton (and now the exceptionally large parish of the Forest of Dartmoor) down to relatively tiny patches like Buckland in the Moor and Sampford Spiney. Those which abut upon the Forest tend to radiate from it like the spokes of a wheel, thus enabling Commoners dwelling at some distance from the Forest to reach it without crossing into any other parish. In the extreme case of Ugborough the greater part of the parish is far removed from the Forest, and is connected to it by a narrow corridor a few hundred yards wide.

East Dart valley

The East Dart valley above Postbridge, seen over the dry-stone wall of Archerton Newtake, with Broad Down left and Hartland Moor right, exemplifying Dartmoor's rounded hills and shallow valleys.

Opposite: **The Dartmoor parishes** before the boundary changes of 1987. (Based upon the 1984 Ordnance Survey 1:25000 map with the permission of the Controller of Her Majesty's Stationery Office. © Crown Copyright.)

Tavy Cleave, the deep rocky gorge where the Tavy descends beneath its range of tors towards the border country of western Dartmoor. 553833.

Great Links Tor, standing in a typical hill-top situation half a mile to the north-west of the view-point, Lower Dunna Goat. 551867.

Bogs and Mires

Dartmoor has a high averaqe rainfall, which normally far exceeds the rate of evaporation, and vast reserves of water are retained. The deep and extensive peat bogs (or "fen") which blanket the high plateaux can be likened to a great sponge which soaks up water until it can hold no more. Waterlogging is accentuated by the poor drainage related to low gradients and in some areas by an impervious layer, the "iron pan", formed by leached-out minerals.

Except after periods of excessive rainfall water tends to be released slowly, and only in times of drought does it become easier to walk across the fen, when the *Sphagnum* moss, a sure indicator of particularly wet situations, and a very efficient reservoir in itself, loses its brilliance and turns a creamy white.

A hollow filled with slush and masked by surface vegetation is strictly a "mire" (and not a bog), to which the term "Marsh" is sometimes applied as part of a proper name, if it is of sufficient consequence. Mires are uncomfortable places, to be treated with respect.

Fox Tor Mire, the best-known of the Dartmoor mires. It is thought to have been the model of Conan Doyle's "Grimpen Mire", and became the centre of controversy when the projected Swincombe reservoir to be sited here was being debated. 6170, 6270.

_____ Rivers and Streams _____

Wester Wella Brook, coming down towards its confluence with the Avon, with Huntingdon Warren above the further bank. 666665.

Most of Dartmoor's streams rise in the "great northern morass" around Cranmere Pool, where the highest elevations are reached, and whilst streams are perhaps not so abundant as might be the case on less absorbent terrain, they are numerous even so. Of the main rivers which result from the presence of many little feeders, only the Ockments and the Taw flow towards the North Devon coast; the others - the Tavy, Plym, Yealm, Erme, Avon, Dart and Teign - eventually find their way into the English Channel.

Whilst there must have been long periods during the Ice Ages when the area which is now Dartmoor was covered by ice and snow, there are no natural dams which would have resulted if scouring by ice had deposited moraines in the valleys, so there are no natural lakes (except that on Dartmoor a "lake" is a stream) or even large natural ponds.

The descent of the streams is in general fairly rapid as they cascade over their rocky beds, and there are numerous minor falls such as those on Shavercombe Brook, Doetor Brook and the East Dart. Where there are comparatively substantial cascades like Manga Falls and Becka Falls the streams tend to hide themselves beneath a jumble of boulders unless they are in spate. However, we rarely have to look far to find some quite spectacular scenes.

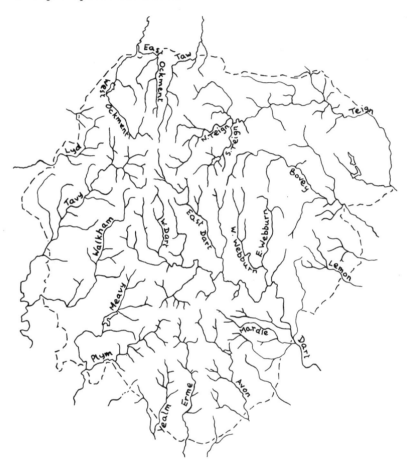

The Dartmoor river systems. The map shows how the basic NW-SE decline of altitude affects the direction of river flow, with the main streams of the Dart dividing the moor in half. (Based upon the 1984 Ordnance Survey 1:25000 map with the permission of the Controller of Her Majesty's Stationery Office © Crown Copyright.)

___ The Tors and Rock-piles ___

On many hilltops, and often on hillside slopes, the tors present a notable and characteristic feature of the landscape; they represent the remnants of a geological system of considerable volume. Tors are more numerous on the northern moor, but from most directions of approach the frontier heights are dominated by some fine examples, such as the well-known trio of Hay Tor, Saddle and Rippon Tors above the eastern fringe, and Sourton Tors to the west.

Though rock-piles are typically of granite, some of those near the edge of the moor are of metamorphic rock. A good example of a non-granite (metamorphosed basic igneous "greenstone") tor is Cocks Tor (Peter Tavy, 530762).

The granite, being igneous, exhibits none of the stratification which is seen in the shales, slates and sandstones which surround it, and from which the metamorphic aureole was formed. It possesses, however, planes of weakness which manifest themselves in a variety of ways. The rock tends to separate at these planes, producing "false bedding" - and an infinite variety of rock formations.

During the process of fragmentation, debris has moved down the hillsides, resulting in rock-fields of often highly concentrated density, known as "clitters".

✦

Saddle Tor (Ilsington, 751763), near the Bovey Tracey-Widecombe road between Haytor Rocks and Rippon Tor, is an "avenue" tor (of which there are many), in this case consisting of two main piles separated by a wide expanse of turf.

Great Mis Tor (Forest/Walkhampton, 562769). A massive tor with extensive clitter, overlooking the Walkham $\frac{1}{2}$ mile north-east of Merivale.

Saddle Tor

Great Mis Tor

Great Staple Tor

Vixen Tor

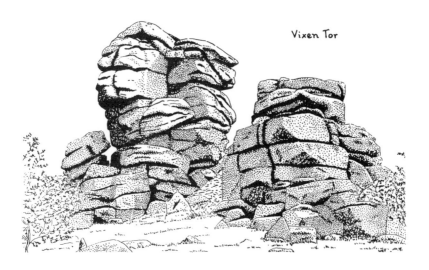

Great Staple (Steeple) Tor (Whitchurch, 543760), on a ridge above the right bank of the Walkham ½ mile NNW of Merivale; this is an avenue tor with some impressive pillars (or "steeples") of rock which Worth called the "Colossi". Mid and Little Staple Tors are on the slope of the hill to the SSW.

Vixen Tor (Whitchurch, 542742) is a formation of striking sphinxlike appearance 1200 yards SW of Merivale Bridge, within enclosures above the right bank of the Walkham. The names of creatures have been applied to several tors and rock-piles, e.g. Fox, Hart, Hare, Doe and Hen Tors, and Eagle and Raven Rocks.

Hound Tor

Hound Tor (Manaton, 742790). A very impressive cluster of rock masses separated by a complex of avenues, Hound Tor has attracted over the years (owing partly no doubt to its proximity to the border country) many imaginative and graphic descriptions; the most obvious relates to its name, which reflects its fancied resemblance to a pack of hounds in full cry.

Fur Tor

One of the piles of **Fur Tor** (Forest, 588831), a widespread complex of rock-piles, situated in a remote area of the northern moor, and peninsulated by some of the tributaries of the Tavy.

✦

Hangershell Rock (Harford, 655593), near the track of the old Red Lake Railway 1200 yards from Harford Moor Gate, overlooks the valley of Butterbrook.

Littaford Tor (Forest, 615770). Several small piles above the left bank of the West Dart in the vicinity of Wistman's Wood. The drawing illustrates some very regular parting.

Little Mis Tor (Walkhampton, 564763), standing 700 yards SSE of Great Mis Tor, looks a little precarious from this angle, quite different from its very square, if diminutive profile, when seen from the Tavistock-Two Bridges road.

Hangershell Rock

Littaford Tor

Little Mis Tor

Crow Tor

Crow Tor (Forest, 606787) is north of the confluence of Foxholes Water and the West Dart, 2.5 miles above Two Bridges. It has been suggested that it takes its name from the resemblance of its most conspicuous pile, when seen from the appropriate angle, to a crouching bird.

━━━━━━━━━━ ✦ ━━━━━━━━━━

Heltor Rock, on enclosed land 1 mile WNW of the village of Bridford, is high above the Teign, and commands extensive views over East Devon. It is accessible by footpath from the road to the south. (Bridford, 790870).

The Puggie (or Puckie) Stone is a massive lump of rock in a private garden by the road from Chagford to Leigh Bridge. (Chagford, 684876).

Blackingstone Rock is about a mile east of Moretonhampstead. Worth described it as perhaps the finest example of a dome-shaped tor, and compared the lamellar but apparently unbroken mass seen from this side with an alternative view of the same rock exhibiting very distinct vertical and horizontal jointing. (Bridford, 787856).

Heltor Rock

The Puggie Stone

Blackingstone Rock

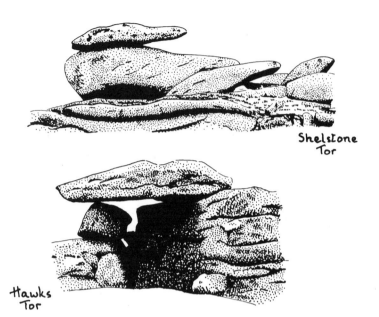

Shelstone
Tor

Hawks
Tor

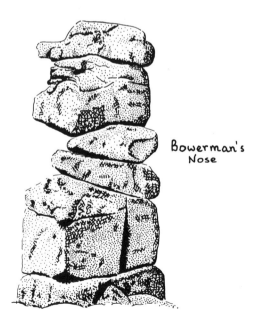

Bowerman's
Nose

Shelstone Tor (Bridestowe and Sourton, 557898) is on the north-west spur of Corn Ridge, between Corn Hole and the West Okement. Its name, like others such as Shilstone and Hangershell, is probably derived from "shelf-stone".

Hawks Tor (Shaugh Prior, 553625) is a cluster of small piles on Wotter Common, 600 yards ENE of Beatland Corner. The chamber-like arrangement seen here gives the impression of artificiality, and was once thought to be a dolmen (see page 88). There has obviously been some interference with the roof slab, but it can be seen to be analogous with the adjacent rocks.

Bowerman's Nose (Manaton, 741804), on Hayne Down, east of the road from Swallerton Gate to Manaton, is a minor formation but attracts attention because of its conspicuously discrete idol-like appearance. The derivation of its name remains unsolved, although it has given rise to much speculation. Seen from another angle, it exemplifies the dramatic change in appearance of most rock-piles when seen from a different view-point.

Blakey Tor is on the north slope of Royal Hill, overlooking the Blackabrook. The transient nature of the granite formations (on a geological time-scale) is well seen in examples such as this. (Forest, 613736).

Bowerman's Nose

Blakey Tor

Saddle Tor - a considerable overhang resulting from a collapse of rock from beneath.

Looka (Lug, Lucky) Tor (Widecombe, 685720) is on the left bank of the Dart by the outfall of a small feeder that comes down from Eastern Combe. The detail in the illustration shows some regular jointing and vertical separation.

Pil Tor (Widecombe, 734759) is a small avenue tor on Tor Hill, 800 yards WSW of White (or Hemsworthy) Gate.

Overleaf
A rock formation at Hound Tor. A common occurrence of horizontal and angled jointing.

Parted rocks - Roos Tor (Peter Tavy, 543766), illustrating the separation which precedes collapse. It is sometimes possible to recognise, in a jumble of boulders, the matching components of a fragmented structure.

The Rundlestone. Rundlestone (or Rendlestone) Tor is by the road that runs from Rundlestone Corner to the TV station on North Hessary Tor. Worth speculated on the probability that this massive slab (reduced by stone workers) is the stone referred to as a Forest boundary mark, and drew a parallel between its two rock basins and the "roundels" of heraldry. Walkhampton, 576746.

Watern Tor, a fine example of a lamellar formation, consists of a series of small masses, running more or less N-S, above the right bank of Walla Brook (N. Teign) 1/2 mile below its source. The two northern piles, when seen from certain angles, give the impression of a single pile pierced by a large aperture - the Thirlstone, an ancient Forest bondmark.

Cuckoo Rock (Walkhampton, 585687) stands conspicuously.sly on the south-west slope of Combeshead Tor, above the right bank of Narrator Brook. It is easily approached by the Middleworth and Deancombe track.

Branscombe's (Bronescombe's) Loaf (Bridestowe and Sourton, 553891) is one of the many lesser rock masses sufficiently distinctive to have been given a name. Its particular relevance, along with a smaller rock nearby (together known as Branscombe's Loaf and Cheese) is in connection with a well-known legend (Gordon, Ruth St. Leger 1965).

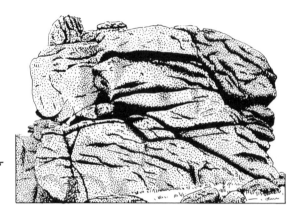

Horizontal and
angled jointing
- Hound Tor

Parked
rocks -
Roos Tor

Massive
slab of
rock -
Rundlestone Tor

The Thurlestone –
Watern Tor

Cuckoo Rock –
from two angles

Branscombe's Loaf

Fallen rock basin
– Cumston Tor

Parted rocks
– Ock Tor

Rock formation
– Roos Tor

Combestone (Cumston) Tor (Holne, 670718) is at the roadside between Holne and Hexworthy, overlooking Dartmeet. The basin on the surface of the fallen rock was formed when it lay horizontally at the summit of the pile.

Parted rocks at Ock (Oke) Tor (Forest, 612899). The separation of the rocks seen here, with slabs resting on them, illustrates the beginning of a process which goes on to create "doorways" of sometimes quite dramatic appearance.

On **Roos Tor, Hound Tor, Thornworthy Tor** (Chagford, 664852) and many other tors, are rocks which, by erosion, are losing support from beneath.

A balanced rock — Thornworthy Tor

Balanced rocks — Hound Tor

The Rugglestone

The Rugglestone (Widecombe, 723746), many years ago adopted as a manor boundary mark, is one of the rocks of a small tor adjacent to an enclosure wall to the south of Southway. The least intrusive approach is from the moor to the east, but it is boggy. The Rugglestone is one of two massive rocks which were once so delicately balanced that they could be rocked with very little effort. They no longer move.

Logan stone
Black Tor

On **Black Tor** (Walkhampton, 573718) there is a boulder which in 1977 I was able to "see-saw", and it was therefore a true "logan-stone". There was a vertical movement of about 3 inches at the ends, but it has since settled into an immobile condition. There are many other notable logans (e.g. The Hangingstone, on the hill of the same name) which no longer rock, and there are many rocking stones insufficiently large to attract attention.

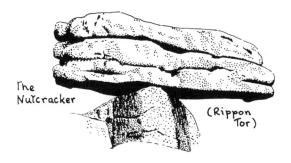

The Nutcracker (Ashburton, 743753) stood near the Ilsington boundary on the slope to the south-west of Rippon Tor, and was clearly visible from the road and adjacent moorland in the vicinity of White Gate. The most familiar and cherished of all the Dartmoor logan-stones, it had long ceased to rock when it was blown up by vandals in 1975. Another Nutcracker, on Sharp Tor, Lustleigh, was levered from its position many years ago.

Logan-stone in the Teign (Drewsteignton, 723897). This massive boulder, which no longer rocks, lies near the left bank of the river, opposite the upstream end of the island below Hunter's Tor. The outline I have drawn from Samuel Prout's sketch of 1806 illustrates the exaggeration employed in past times to dramatise such features. Assuming that the two figures represent average adult males, the rock would be about 20 feet from top to bottom, whereas in fact it is approximately 8 feet high. (Full details of its measurements are to be found in Rowe's *Perambulation*).

____ The Dartmoor Granite ____

Scientists have estimated that about 430 million years ago the earliest rocks still evident in Devon were being laid down under a primeval sea. The granite of what is now the south-west peninsula was formed when a massive upheaval, about 290 million years ago, caused the formation of a gigantic mountain range. It could be said that granite is a rock which cooled and solidified from a molten state under great pressure, a circumstance relating to the weight of the pre-existing sedimentary rocks above it.

The structure of the Dartmoor granite is complicated in places (particularly round its margins) by the effect of overlying rocks falling into it and altering its composition, and by changes occurring within it, during the cooling-down process. It is these factors, bearing on the variation in each of its three main constit-uents (quartz, mica and felspar) which give the granite its range of texture and colour.

Quartz is a glassy grey material which, when broken down, forms the main constituent of sand; it occasionally occurs as amethyst. The gravelly "growan", which is often found underfoot where turf or peat has been removed, is mostly quartz, and results from the decay of the surface granite.

Mica is glittering and usually black (biotite), but white mica (muscovite) occurs in some places as a replacement for felspar; this greying (or greisening) of the granite was one of the changes that came about by chemical action during cooling. Occasionally, near the edges of the moor, biotite has been replaced by tourmaline, which is also black, but is recognised by the presence of fine parallel grooving.

Felspar (or feldspar) in its usual white state occurs in grey granite, but it may be pink, resulting in red granite.

The stone usually seen on the surface, and which typically occurs in the form of tors and rock-piles is Tor granite or Giant granite. It is coarse-grained, with large crystals of quartz and felspar (the latter 1 - 2 inches in length), and may contain xenoliths (rocks which fell into it whilst it was still molten).

Quarry or Blue granite is an underlying type; it is finer-grained, and the crystals of felspar are fewer and smaller (up to $\frac{3}{4}$ inch in length). The very fine-grained Aplites are a third, minor division, some of which arrived later than the Tor and Quarry granites.

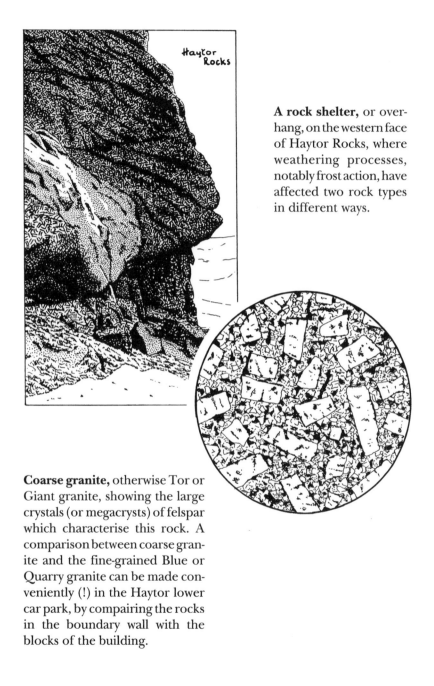

A rock shelter, or overhang, on the western face of Haytor Rocks, where weathering processes, notably frost action, have affected two rock types in different ways.

Coarse granite, otherwise Tor or Giant granite, showing the large crystals (or megacrysts) of felspar which characterise this rock. A comparison between coarse granite and the fine-grained Blue or Quarry granite can be made conveniently (!) in the Haytor lower car park, by compairing the rocks in the boundary wall with the blocks of the building.

Rock basins

A localised weathering process, induced by trapped water, and by frost and wind, has caused the formation of depressions or "rock basins". The erosive process takes place naturally on horizontal surfaces, where they are very common, but they are particularly interesting when seen as indicators of rock movement. The example at Combestone Tor which I have illustrated (see page 36) is but one of many cases which demonstrate the downfall of the topmost member of a pile. The two rock basins on the large slab of rock at Rundlestone Tor lie at different angles, a circumstance brought about by a natural change in the angle at which the rock has rested.

◆

Rock basins - some variations on a theme. The large rock-basin on **Gutter Tor** (Sheepstor, 578668) has a naturally-occurring drainage channel. On **Arms Tor** (Bridestowe and Sourton/Lydford, 540863) there is a small one with an overhanging rim.

The well-known rock-basin on **Great Mis Tor** (Forest/ Walkhampton, 562769), generally assumed to be "Mistor Pan", an ancient Forest boundary mark, once had a bridge across its open end, a unique formation long since vandalised.

The largest rock-basin on the moor, on **Castor rock** (Chagford, 665863), was once surrounded by an iron railing, to prevent sheep falling in, so it is said, but in view of the existence of many other and much more serious hazards without such safeguards this can hardly have been a valid reason.

The holed stone in the Teign (Gidleigh, 655870) lies downstream from Teignever Bridge. The hole in this massive boulder was obviously caused by trapped pebbles activated by the motion of the stream.

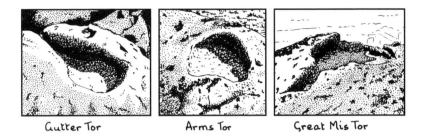

Gutter Tor   Arms Tor   Great Mis Tor

Rock basins

Kestor

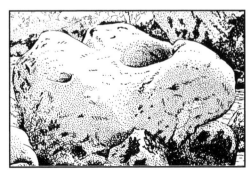

The holed stone in the
Teign below Scorhill.

Caves

The limestone caves on the edge of the National Park at Buckfastleigh are of considerable scientific interest. However, on the moors there is nothing on a similar scale. There is the occasional semblance of a cave caused by the disposition of rocks, resulting from the natural processes of tor disintegration, but even the most cave-like and best-known examples, of which the Pixies' Cave on Sheeps Tor is one, are very restricted in size.

There are various classes of man-made caves, including the "potato caves" associated with farmsteads, and the "beehive huts" of the early tinners, which will be mentioned later.

The soil

The activities of man over very many centuries, which have been largely responsible for changes in vegetation, notably clearance by cutting and burning, and by grazing, have combined with changing patterns of climate to influence the development of the present soil structure. The result is that, over a substratum of granite, growan and head, there lie areas of peaty soils and brown earths. (Head consists of a layer of rock-waste soil resulting from earth flows caused by brief warm spells alternating with the long cold periods of the Ice Ages.)

The peaty soils of the high moors, which result from saturated conditions, and where the rainfall is over 80 inches a year, are known as peaty gleys. Sloping away from these areas of blanket bog is a band, of variable width, of loamy soils called peaty-gleyed podsols where from a black surface layer the minerals in the soil have leached out, tending to create a barrier in the form of an iron pan; this causes waterlogging.

The brown earths occur mainly on the eastern side, and particularly over a large area around Moretonhampstead, where the altitude is between 750 and 1100 feet, and the annual rainfall is about 35-50 inches.

Some of these effects can be seen in the many small roadside quarries which were excavated for road-building materials.

Part II
FLORA AND FAUNA

The subject of Dartmoor's natural history is of course virtually infinite, and there is a correspondingly comprehensive literature. If I had to select one volume as a general review I would choose the very readable account written by Harvey and Gordon for the "New Naturalist" library; it includes some extensive species lists.

I can only treat the subject briefly, and mention a few species which I feel to be characteristic, with a bias towards the higher levels of the moor. As related subjects, I have included mention of livestock and commercial softwoods.

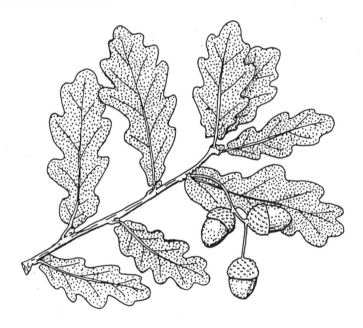

The **Pedunculate Oak** (*Quercus robur*), the common oak of Devon and Dartmoor, normally has long stalks to its acorns and short leaf-stalks. The less common species, the Durmast or Sessile Oak (*Quercus petraea*), usually has sessile acorns and long leaf-stalks.

Vegetation

A glance through the *Atlas of the Devon Flora* (Ivimey-Cook, 1984) will give a clear indication of those plants for which high Dartmoor is a distinctly favoured habitat. These include Cross-leaved Heath and Ling, Whortleberry, Heath Rush, Purple Moor-grass, Mat-grass, Bog-cotton, Deer-grass, and many others. There are numerous Devon flowers which are totally absent, and there are some, such as Wood Sorrel, Soft Rush and Sweet Vernal-grass, which show neither a marked preference for, nor intolerance of the moorland scene, being generally distributed over much of Dartmoor and the rest of the county in suitable places.

The kind of ground cover in any one locality is dependent not only upon the natural factors of altitude and climate, the chemistry of the soil and its wetness (and dryness here is to an extent only comparative), but also, and very significantly, upon land management. Grazing and swaling (the burning of old vegetation, useless as stock feed, to make way for fresh young growth) are important among these factors, and will change the balance of a plant community. One of the effects of persistent swaling is that Purple Moor-grass *(Molinia)*, unattractive to livestock, tends to become dominant over extensive areas.

There are those plants which are so common and widespread over particular stretches of countryside that these areas can be conveniently classified according to the dominant kinds of vegetation, under the headings of grass-, heather-, bracken- and whortleberry-moor, in addition to the blanket bogs of the upland plateaux, and the mires and marshes.

Wildflowers

I have drawn a representative selection of wildflowers, most of which are particularly relevant to the high moors; and there are many others which come into this category, though not confined to a moorland habitat, for example the Sheep's Sorrel *(Rumex acetosella)*, a common creeping dock with small halberd-shaped leaves, and Water Blinks *(Montia fontana)*, a pale little plant with tiny flowers.

Coming down to lower levels we grade into an area still within the National Park but more akin to the surrounding countryside, and the flower list becomes very extensive. Such an area is the north-eastern sector, where the wild Daffodil grows along the banks of the Teign. And wherever we happen to be there are plants which attract our attention, such as the occasional Welsh Poppy *(Meconopsis cambrica)*, the roadside Marjoram *(Origanum vulgare)*, the flamboyant and increasing Himalayan Balsam *(Impatiens glandulifera)*, the little Opposite-leaved Golden Saxifrage *(Chrysosplenium oppositifolium)* of wet shady places, Pink Purslane *(Montia sibirica)*, introduced and increasing on banks, in hedges and on shady streamsides, not to be confused with Water Purslane *(Lythrum portula)* of wet heath and bog, and Thyme-leaved Speedwell *(Veronica serpyllifolia)* of wet heaths and grassland. The woodlands, the roadside verges, the stone-built hedges, the little valley-bogs (many of them easily accessible), each have their particular plant communities.

Some moorland flowers

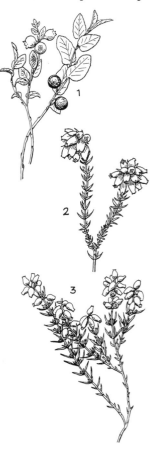

1. **Whortleberry** *(Vaccinium myrtillus)*, widespread and common within the National Park, is found in a wide range of situations, though preferring drier habitats. It is in some places a dominant qround-cover plant, and the harvesting of its fruits ("hurts") for sale was once a common activity.

2. **Cross-leaved Heath** *(Erica tetralix)*, which prefers a damp habitat, is recognisable by its terminal clusters of pale rose-coloured bells, and by the arrangement of its leaves, in whorls of four.

3. **Bell Heather** *(E.cinerea)* occurs in drier locations. It has slender reddish-purple bells, less compactly arranged than those of the cross-leaved species, and leaves in whorls of three, with small clusters in the axils.

4. **Common Heath** or **Ling** *(Calluna vulgaris)* prefers well-drained soil; it is widespread and often abundant, carpeting large areas like Headland Warren and Soussons Down in late summer. It bears spikes of small pale-purple flowers and has minute densely-overlapping leaves, arranged in four rows along the branches.

5. **Lousewort** *(Pedicularis sylvatica)*, with its rosy-coloured flowers on decumbent stems, occurs quite commonly on damp moorland and poor pasture. In olden times it took the blame for the attacks of parasites on sickly stock grazing under such conditions - whence its common name.

6. **Heath Bedstraw** *(Galium saxatile)*, a common plant of moor and grassland, weak and low-growing, with whorls of short elliptical leaves and small white 4-petalled flowers.

7. **Heath Milkwort** *(Polygala serpyllifolia)*. A small attractive plant of moor and grassland, with flowers of variable shade, usually blue. Its generic name derives from the greek *polus* and *gala* (much milk), from an ancient idea that it improved the milk production of cows.

8. **Eyebright** *(Euphrasia)*, a small plant of moor and grassland, with white purple-streaked flowers. There are numerous species, several of which occur on Dartmoor; they are said to be partially parasitic on the roots of other plants.

9. **Tormentil** *(Potentilla erecta)*, a very common plant with bright yellow flowers. There are three relevant species, of which *P.erecta* is the most typical at the higher levels. There are usually four petals, occasionally five, and rarely six.

10. **Western Furze** (or **Gorse**) *(Ulex gallii)* may be seen flowering at almost any season but it flowers mainly about July-September. This species is characterised by its low growth and curved spines. Its relative, the European Gorse, flowers generally earlier (about March-June), has a much taller habit, and bears long straight spines.

Some plants found in wet situations _____

1. **Marsh St. John's-wort** *(Hypericum elodes)* is a densely-hairy plant with creeping or floating stems and yellow flowers on erect branches. Its close relatives e.g. Slender St. John's-wort *(H.pulchrum)* and creeping St. John's-wort *(H.humifusum)* grow in dry habitats.

2. **Lenormand's Water-crowfoot** *(Ranunculus omiophyllus)* grows in pools and running water; it has white flowers. Ivy-leaved water crowfoot *(R.hederaceus)* also occurs, but less commonly.

3. **Round-leaved Sundew** *(Drosera rotundifolia)* is common in bogs. It feeds on insects, which are caught by means of sticky red hairs on its yellowish-green leaves, and provide nutrients unobtainable from the acid, peaty soil. It has small white flowers. Another species, Long-leaved Sundew *(D.intermedia)* occurs rarely on Dartmoor.

4 and 5. **Cotton-grass** or **Bog-cotton** *(Eriophorum)*. The bog-cottons are in fact rush-like sedges. Their small flower-heads develop into white cottony tufts, often forming dense snowy carpets over boggy terrain. **Hare's-tail** *(E.vaginatum)* (4) is easily recognised by its single erect head, whereas **Common Cotton-grass** *(E.angustifolium)* (5) has clusters of nodding heads.

6. **Pale Butterwort** *(Pinguicula lusitanica)* is another bog-dwelling insectivorous plant. This species traps its prey on its sticky leaves, which curl their edges over its captures. It has small lilac-coloured flowers.

7. **Bog Asphodel** *(Narthecium ossifragum)* has starry yellow flowers. Its specific name, *ossifragum*, means bone-breaking, an allusion to its reputation of causing brittle bones in livestock, a condition no doubt more justifiably attributable to the generally poor quality of the grazing where the plant grows.

8. **Bog Pimpernel** *(Anagallis tenella)* grows in bogs and other wet or damp situations. It is a prostrate plant with pairs of small oval leaves and pink bell-shaped flowers.

9. **Ivy-leaved Bell-flower** *(Wahlenbergia hederacea)*. This enchanting little plant with its pale blue flowers grows in wet places, particularly near streams.

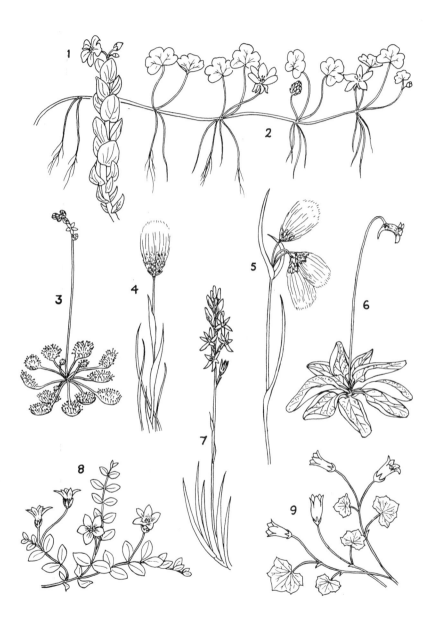

Some plants of woods, walls and moorland ___

1. **Common Cow-wheat** *(Melampyrum pratense)* grows in woods, on banks and in shady places; it also occurs in open country. It is a floppy semi-parasitic plant with lanceolate leaves and pairs of pale flowers, usually yellow, sometimes pinkish-mauve.

2. **Wall Pennywort** or **Navelwort** *(Umbilicus rupestris)*, with its spikes of greenish-white flowers, is a typical species of walls, stone-built hedges and other rocky places.

3. **Wood Sage** *(Teucrium scorodonia)* is generally distributed in suitably well-drained situations. It is a labiate with pairs of greenish-yellow flowers on branched spikes.

4. **English Stonecrop** *(Sedum anlicum)* is widespread and common in dry places. It has starry white flowers, tinged with pink.

5. **Wood Sorrel** *(Oxalis acetosella)* has white flowers, streaked with pink, and is widely distributed in shady places, except in the wettest situations.

6. **Heath Spotted Orchid** *(Dactylorhiza maculata* ssp. *ericetorum)* grows in damp locations. Its flowers are variable in colour, ranging from white to shades of purple, but they are generally pale with darker streaks or dots.

7. **Goldenrod** *(Solidago virgaurea)* is seen occasionally in dry situations from the fringe woodlands to the high moors. It has branched spikes of bright yellow flowers.

Some more plants of wet situations _____

1. **Water Forget-me-not.** Three similar species of Water Forget me-not occur in Devon; the most widespread on Dartmoor is *Myosotis secunda.* The flowers of this group of plants are blue with yellow centres, and open in succession as the stalk lengthens, the latter developing a curl (hence another name for the genus - Scorpion-grass).

2. **Lesser Spearwort** *(Ranunculus flammula)* is a tall-stemmed relative of the buttercups (although it doesn't look like one in its early stages). Found in bogs and marshes, it is equally at home both on and off the moor.

3. **Bog Violet** *(Viola palustris)* has white creeping stems and dark-veined lilac-coloured flowers; it is found in bogs, and in wet places on heaths and in woodlands.

4. **Bog Pondweed** *(Potamogeton polygonifolius)*, by far the commonest member of the genus, occurs in pools and in slow streams. Its leaves are of two shapes; those submerged are lanceolate, whilst the floating leaves are elliptical. The small flowers grow densely on a stout stalk.

5. **Marsh Pennywort** *(Hydrocotyle vulgaris)* is a common plant with a creeping stem and disc-shaped leaves, its tiny flowers arising from the bases of the leaf-stalks.

6. **Marsh Willow-herb** *(Epilobium palustre)* is more likely to be seen on Dartmoor than other members of the genus. It has narrow leaves and drooping buds giving rise to rose-lilac flowers.

7. **Red Rattle** *(Pedicularis palustris)* is related to Lousewort, but grows in wetter places and is far less common; it also stands taller and looks much more robust. It has pink and crimson flowers and toothed pinnate leaves.

8. **Lesser Skullcap** *(Scutellaria minor)* is a small plant with slender stem and pale pink tubular flowers which give the impression of growing in pairs.

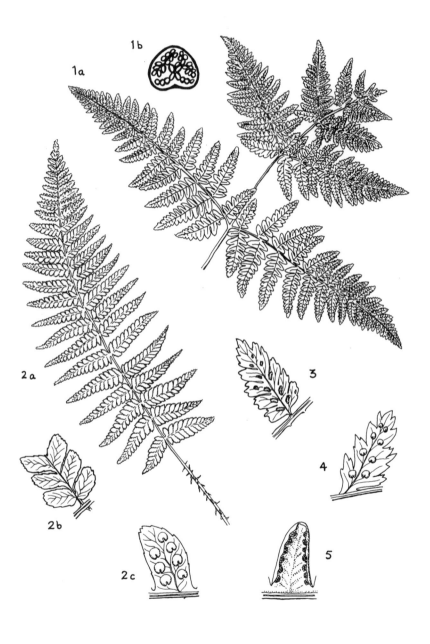

Bracken and ferns

1a. **Bracken** *(Pteridium aquilinum)* is a serious pest, widespread and abundant, increasingly eliminating extensive areas of grazing by replacing grass and heather. Whilst it is a fern, both strictly and colloquially, it is not invariably accepted as one - its coarse habit, when exposed on the open moor, and troublesome effect, tend to separate it from the delicate and graceful plants more affectionately regerded as ferns.

1b. A section through the underground stem of Bracken, illustrating the pattern (progressively variable in detail) formed by the woody tissue. The are several fanciful interpretations of this design. The most pertinent of them is that it resembles a double-headed or spread-eagle, because it is from this idea that the plant takes its scientific name *(aquilinum* - to do with eagles).

2a. **Male Fern** *(Dryopteris filix-mas)* is common almost everywhere, in suitable locations, such as by walls, on roadside verges, in open situations and waste places, and in woods.

2b. The identification of ferns is sometimes aided by the examination of small details. This drawing shows the shape of a Male Fern pinnule.

2c. The underside of a lobe showing the arrangement - the capsules containing the spores.

3. **Lady Fern** *(Athyrium filix-femina)* is a common and variable species typically found in damp woods and at the sides of streams. Lobe and spore capsules.

4. **Broad Buckler-fern** *(Dryopteris dilatata)* is to be found in a wide range of situations, including the high moors. Lobe and spore capsules.

5. **Lemon-scented** or **Mountain Fern** *(Oreopteris limbosperma)* produces a smell of citrus from small globular glands on the backs of the fronds when rubbed. It is found chiefly in association with flowing water, notably in high woodlands, and shows a distinct preference for Dartmoor, being unrecorded for most of the rest of Devon. Lobe and spore capsules.

Ferns

1. **Harts-tongue** *(Phyllitis scolopendrium)* has long strap-like leaves (the only fern with undivided leaves). It is confined to shady places, and so is found more in woods and in shady rocky situations.

2. **Polypody** *(Polypodium vulgare)*, with its long pinnately-divided leaves, is a common plant of walls and rocks, and also grows as an epiphyte on trees; it is seen to great effect, for example, on the stunted oaks of Wistman's Wood.

3. **Maidenhair Spleenwort** *(Asplenium trichomanes)*. commonly seen on walls and rocks, has pairs of small oval or oblong leaflets on long wiry stalks.

4. **Black Spleenwort** *(A. adiantum-nigrum)*, another fern to be found on walls and rocks, has triangular much-divided leaves on black stalks.

5. **Hard Fern** *(Blechnum spicant)* is generally distributed in well-drained habitats. The fronds are of two types - the lower fronds are spreading and barren, whilst the upper fronds are longer, erect, with narrow pinnae, and are spore-bearing.

Mosses

Mosses, together with the liverworts and lichens, make a very important contribution to the plant life of this upland region. There are very many species, and the identification of all these groups is in general an undertaking for the specialist.

The *Polytrichum* species are among the most noticeable of the mosses, and the walker cannot fail to be familiar with *Sphagnum*, which occurs to the exclusion of most other plants in the wettest places. The most frequent replacement for *Sphagnum*, where the terrain becomes less wet, is *Hypnum cupressiforme* (Cypress-leaved Feather-moss), and there are several species which are fairly constant within their various habitats. These include *Dicranum scoparium* (Lesser Fork-moss), and the Feather-mosses *Pleurosium schreberi*, *Rhytidiadelphus squarrosus*, and *Hylocomium splendens*.

A "luminous" (i.e. highly reflective) moss, *Schistostega*, is sometimes seen in the dark crevices of rock-piles.

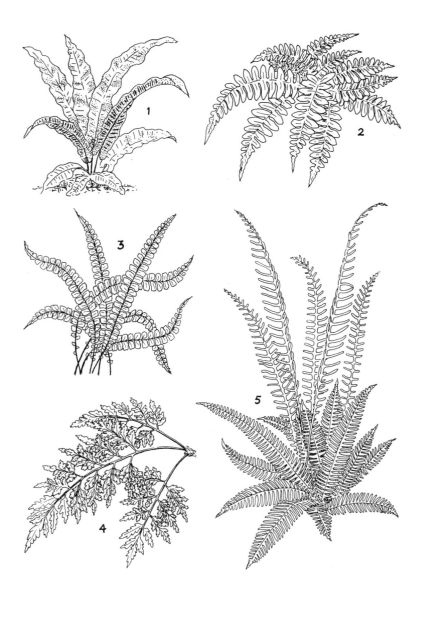

Some characteristic rushes, grasses and sedges

Rushes

Soft Rush *(Juncus effusus)*
Heath Rush *(J.squarrosus)*
Toad Rush *(J.bufonius)*
Bulbous Rush *(J.bulbosus)*
Sharp-flowered Rush
  (J.acutiflorus)
Jointed Rush *(J.articulatus)*
Field Woodrush
  (Luzula campestris)
Many-headed Woodrush
  (L.multiflora)
Greater Woodrush *(L.sylvatica)*

Grasses

Red Fescue *(Festuca rubra)*
Sheep's Fescue *(F.ovina)*
Rye-grass *(Lolium perenne)*
Annual Meadow-grass
  (Poa annua)
Cock's-foot *(Dactylis glomerata)*
Crested Dog's-tail
  (Cynosurus cristatus)
Floating Sweet-grass
  (Glyceria fluitans)
Soft Brome
  (Bromus hordeaceus)
False Oat
  (Arrhenatherum elatius)
Tufted Hair-grass
  (Deschampsia caespitosa)
Wavy Hair-grass *(D.flexuosa)*
Early Hair-grass *(Aira praecox)*
Silver Hair-grass
(A. caryophyllea)

Sweet Vernal-grass
  (Anthoxanthum odoratum)
Yorkshire Fog *(Holcus lanatus)*
Creeping Soft-grass *(H.mollis)*
Brown Bent-grass
  (Agrostis canina)
Heath Bent-grass *(A.curtisii)*
Common Bent-grass
  (A.capillaris)
Creeping Bent-grass
  (A.stolonifera)
Heath Grass
  (Danthonia decumbens)
Purple Moor-grass
  (Molinia caerulea)
Mat-grass *(Nardus stricta)*

Sedges

Deer-grass
  (Trichophorum cespitosum)
Common Cotton-grass
  (Eriophorum angustifolium)
Hare's-tail Cotton-grass
  (E.vaginatum)
Many-stemmed Spike-rush
  (Eleocharis multicaulis)
Oval Sedge *(Carex ovalis)*
Star Sedge *(C.echinata)*
Carnation Grass *(C.panicea)*
Ribbed Sedge *(C.binervis)*
Common Yellow-sedge
  (C.demissa)
Pill-headed Sedge *(C.pilulifera)*
Common Sedge *(C.nigra)*

Fungi, liverworts and lichens *(illustrated overleaf)*

1. **Coprophilous fungi.** The varied habitats of Dartmoor, from the border woodlands to the heaths and *Sphagnum* bogs of the higher terrain, all have their particular fungus communities. Animal dung, which is liberally distributed over the grazing land, provides a convenient situation for a rich fungus-flora, and several genera (e.g. *Coprinus* and *Paneolus*) contain species which flourish on the nutrients there.

Dung is so transient a medium that growth from a long-living fungal mycelium is not possible. It is likely, therefore, that these organisms arise directly from spores, quite probably ingested by animals and voided in their droppings.

2. **Liverworts** are closely related to mosses, and the division between them is not always clear. As a group they are more dependent on water, and tolerant of shade. The "leafy" liverworts, with their fleshy lobed fronds, are widely distributed, and may abound in almost any saturated situation.

3-8. **Lichens.** These plants are able to occupy kinds of habitat for which there may be little or no competition, and on Dartmoor the rock-piles, clitters and field-boundaries offer habitats in good measure. In addition, they share other situations with ferns, mosses and liverworts, as for example on the trees in the valley woods and upland copses.

It is possibly superficially to confuse lichens with mosses, but many may be distinguished by their cup-like fruiting-bodies. A lichen is unique in that it is a composite organism, comprising a fungus and an alga, living together in a delicately balanced state of symbiosis. The fungus element is dependent upon the alga to survive because it needs a supply of organic food which is manufactured by the alga; many lichen algae, on the other hand, are also free living.

Lichens occur in three basic forms, distinguishable by their general appearance and the way in which they are attached.

3 and 4. **Foliose** lichens are leaf- or scale-like, and are attached by root-like threads; the specimens illustrated here are growing on wood *(Parmelia)* and among grass *(Peltigera)*.

5. A beard-lichen (*Usnea*), a genus of **fruticose** lichens; these are bush- or tassel-like, and attached at the base.

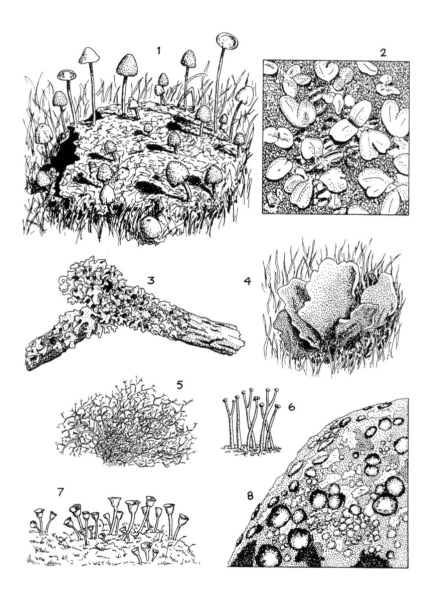

8. A rock surface covered with **crustose** lichens. These crustaceous species are closely attached by the whole under-surface; the upper surface is often divided into little more-or-less hexagonal areas.

6 and 7. Fruiting-bodies, or **apothecia** of lichens. These forms are known as "Dartmoor matchsticks" and "Pixy cups" (*Cladonia* spp.). Lichens also reproduce vegetatively.

Lichens are very important members of Dartmoor's plant community. They are also very slow-growing. As an example of this, I compared the photograph by R.H.Worth of a kistvaen on Stennen Hill, published in 1938 (TDA Vol.70), with my photograph taken some thirty years later, and could detect no obvious difference in the lichen pattern. But these organisms are very sensitive to atmospheric pollution, and herein lies a situation where the by-products of our modern way of life could have a disastrous effect.

Trees and woodlands

The amount of tree cover that Dartmoor may have once supported is open to question. The demands of the local population and the industries of the past would have made considerable inroads into what timber there was, not to mention the need for oak in the days of wooden fighting ships. Native hardwoods are now seen at their best only in the beautiful valley woodlands of the border country, where the Pedunculate Oak *(Quercus robur)* is the dominant species.

There are now only three small areas of indigenous oak-wood on the high moors:

Wistman's Wood (Forest, 612772), on the east (left) bank of the West Dart, $1\frac{1}{4}$ miles to the north of Two Bridges.

Piles Wood (or Copse) (Harford, 644620), on the east (left) bank of the Erme, $1\frac{1}{2}$ miles to the north of Harford church.

Black Tor Beare (or Copse) (Okehampton, 566890), on the east (right) bank of the West Ockment a mile upstream from Meldon Reservoir.

Extensive tree cover on high Dartmoor now takes the form of conifer plantations. Apart from the rowans and one or two other species which favour sheltered sites such as the little tributary valleys, and an occasional stunted hawthorn, there are few other trees to be seen on the open moor. That trees were once more widespread has been demonstrated by the presence of roots in the peat - these can sometimes be seen protruding from the banks of moorland streams.

The planting of windbreaks years ago accounts for many of the Beeches which occur in close proximity to human habitations; and trees like the Sycamore and sometimes less characteristic species such as the Scots Pine may be found in the vicinity of outlying farmsteads. (There are no trees on Dartmoor more alien than the conspicuous Monkey-puzzles at Headland Warren.)

A short list of Dartmoor trees

Common Sallow *(Salix cinerea)*
Eared Sallow *(S.aurita)*
Silver Birch *(Betula pendula)*
Alder *(Alnus glutinosa)*
Hazel *(Corylus avellana)*
Beech *(Fagus sylvaticus)*
Pedunculate Oak *(Quercus robur)*

Sessile Oak *(Q.petraea)*
Rowan *(Sorbus aucuparia)*
Hawthorn *(Crataegus monogyna)*
Sycamore *(Acer pseudoplanatus)*
Holly *(Ilex aquifolium)*
European Larch *(Laryx decidua)*
Scots Pine *(Pinus sylvestris)*

Commercial softwoods

The twentieth century tendency to cover large areas of Dartmoor with conifers has shown itself not only in hitherto open country, but also in the replacement of native trees in some of the border valleys.

The plantations which have made the greatest impact, in an open moorland context, are at Fernworthy, Bellever, Soussons Down and Burrator, and there is a scattering of lesser, but nevertheless substantial stands, notably at Brimpts and Beardown.

Some principal timber producers

Norway Spruce *(Picea abies)*
Sitka Spruce *(P.sitchensis)*
Japanese Larch *(Larix leptolepis)*
Douglas Fir *(Pseudotsuga taxifolia)*
Beach or Shore ("Contorta") Pine *(Pinus contorta)*

Leaf-patterns of some typical broad-leaved trees

(illustrated overleaf)

1. **Silver Birch.** A ready coloniser of marginal heathland, this elegant tree prefers a well-lit site, and thus plays an important part in enhancing such scenes as may be obtained from the roadside on Trendlebere Down.

2. **Holly,** a hardwood of frequent occurrence, often among the oak, ash, hazel and other species of the valley woodlands.

3. **Rowan** or **Mountain Ash,** a tree particularly evocative of Dartmoor, is likely to be noticed when it occurs in relative isolation in the valleys and gullies of the open moor, as it so often does, or amongst other trees, by virtue of its white flowers or its red berries.

4. **Sycamore,** a common species, but not native, often found in the vicinity of dwelling-places may, because of its fecundity, propagate itself to an unwelcome extent in woodland conservation sites.

5. **Beech.** The beeches planted as windbreaks and shelter belts in earlier years tend to fall victim to gales and to the timber merchant as they reach maturity, illustrating one of the many changes that can occur in the landscape.

6. **Alder,** once a principal species in the valley woodlands. Its decline was due in part to its popularity during the tinning era as an unrivalled charcoal tree. It is still common, however, in wet marginal situations, notably along river banks.

Animal Life

The high moors are not rich in terms of obvious resident fauna. On the blanket bogs there is little in the way of hospitable cover for most creatures, and because of the saturated nature of the terrain the activities of burrowing species are severely restricted. However, there are some nesting birds, and the faunal lists are extended by the occurrence of many transient species, either with or without distinctly moorland relationships, especially numerous other kinds of birds and of insects.

Increase in numbers and variety naturally occurs with decreasing altitude and a corresponding improvement in habitats. Fluctuations occur, of course; for example, the fluidity of the wild mammal population has been demonstrated by the loss of the Marten and Polecat, and more recently by the effects of myxomatosis on the Rabbit, and the introduction of Mink on the native Otters.

The woods and plantations provide cover for the very numerous **Roe Deer** (*Capreolus capreolus*), and there is a small resident herd of Red Deer (*Cervus elaphus*).

Some common mammals

The **Fox** *(Vulpes vulpes)* is likely to be seen almost anywhere on the moor, maintaining its estimated three or four per square mile by its ability to flourish in a region inhospitable to many other quadrupeds, finding good cover in the gullies and among the rocks. It feeds on small vertebrates, insects, fruit and berries. Rabbits form a substantial proportion of its diet, and in summer very many beetles are taken. Several packs of hounds hunt the moor from their respective quarters around its periphery.

The **Badger** *(Meles meles)* is common and widespread, and although it tends to favour the woodlands its setts can be found in many places out on the open moor. It feeds on a wide range of vegetable and animal material, and I have seen badgers come to a car park for scraps, where they will tolerate the glare of headlights for a short time. (The temptation of the peanut butter sandwich is now almost legendary.) Badgers have a habit of putting in an appearance now and again, but it is perhaps most rewarding to watch for a family group to emerge from its sett.

The **Stoat** *(Mustela erminea)* and its smaller relative, the Weasel *(M.nivalis)* are probably seen most often as they run across an in-country road in front of one's car. They are equally at home, however, on open moorland, where they frequent rough and rocky terrain. (One early morning I watched a family party of Stoats playing among the summit rocks of Rippon Tor, the nearest one raising itself erect from behind a rock and weaving from side to side, apparently mystified by my presence there.)

The **Grey Squirrel** *(Sciurus carolinensis)*, introduced into Britain from 1876 to 1929, is a pest of woodlands, mainly of hardwoods, where damage is inflicted on young trees by stripping bark from their stems. It is common in such habitats, and is also seen occasionally at some distance out onto the moor. A wide variety of vegetable food is taken, largely acorns, and other nuts and seeds, and occasionally small animal matter.

Fox

Badger

Stoat

Grey
Squirrel

Birds

Of the many common birds which frequent the moors, several members of the crow family are likely to be seen there. Skylarks and Meadow Pipits are also common, and we may see an occasional Kestrel or a Heron, a scattering of Peewits, or perhaps a flock of Golden Plover persuaded away from a nearby estuary by a rising tide. But there are some species, like the Buzzard, the Raven, the Dipper, Grey Wagtail, and the Wheatear in its season, which more than most have a special affinity with the moorland scene.

Other species which tend to favour the National Park are the Whinchat, Stonechat and Reed Bunting; and there are four breeding species - the Redstart, Tree Pipit, Wood Warbler and Pied Flycatcher - which are significant in being especially associated with western oak-woods.

Familiar birds are not unusual up to surprisingly high levels (I have seen, for example, a flock of Bluetits in Wistman's Wood), and at the roadside car parks the familiar Chaffinch turns up regularly for food.

Bird populations are constantly changing, and on Dartmoor a contributory factor has been the provision of new habitats in the form of forestry plantations and reservoirs. The former, whilst unattractive to most of the species which are associated with native hardwoods, provide a niche for an alternative, though more restricted population. The reservoirs provide habitats for various water fowl, more particularly in winter, but they are restricted by the lack of shallow-water vegetation.

A matter of concern to ornithologists is excessive human intrusion into the high moors, which threatens the breeding of sensitive species like the Golden Plover (in its only breeding ground in southern England), the Dunlin and the Snipe. There are others, such as the Common Sandpiper (which, like the Dunlin, is at the southern limit of its range) which might breed if sufficiently undisturbed.

Heron *(Ardea cinerea).* A view of a Heron, though not an occasion for surprise, is nevertheless for many of us a special event. It is not a common bird, but its size makes it conspicuous, and it forages into the remotest parts of the moor. Its population tends to fall in severe winters, because of the interruption of its food supply (very varied but largely aquatic). However, it manages to maintain a limited nesting presence within the National Park.

Birds of moors and streams

The **Raven** *(Corvus corax)*, the largest of our crows, can be distinguished from the Carrion Crow by its size, its wedge-shaped tail and its deep croak. The aerobatic displays presented by a couple or sometimes three ravens are a joy to see - a pleasure not shared by the sheep farmer, whose lambs may fall prey to their depredations.

The **Buzzard** *(Buteo buteo)*. The farmer extends this distaste to the Buzzard, a common bird of prey, which is likely to be seen on any excursion to the moors, perhaps at close quarters, but more often soaring high up against the sky.

The **Ring Ouzel** *(Turdus torquatus)*, a summer visitor which returns annually to breed, particularly on the northern moor, and best-known as a frequenter of some of the old tin-workings. It is closely related to the Blackbird, being easily recognised by the white crescent on its breast.

The **Dipper** *(Cinclus cinclus)* may be seen bobbing up and down on a boulder or flying to and from its nest-hole in the bank of a stream. Its diet consists mainly of bottom-dwelling insect larvae, but other small aquatic creatures are also taken, and a little vegetable matter.

The **Wheatear** *(Oenanthe oenanthe)*. Dartmoor is the British breeding stronghold of this summer visitor, which frequents walls and clitter, displaying its vivid white rump when it flies off to a safer distance.

The **Grey Wagtail** *(Motacilla cinerea)*, a beautiful long-tailed bird with grey back and yellow belly, which lives by the streams of the moors and surrounding countryside. The male in summer has a distinctive black throat-patch.

Raven

Buzzard

Ring
Ouzel

Dipper

Wheatear

Grey Wagtail

Nuthatch

Goldcrest

Red Grouse

Whinchat

Curlew

Snipe

Cuckoo

Meadow Pipit

Birds of moors and woods

The **Red Grouse** *(Lagopus lagopus)* occurs sparsely as a breeding bird on the higher moors. Its diet is said to consist mainly of a wide range of moorland plant material, particularly the shoots, flowers and seed heads of the Common Heath.

The **Nuthatch** *(Sitta europaea)* is resident in the vicinity of hardwood trees, where it feeds on acorns, hazel nuts, beechmast and other seeds, and on various insects and other invertebrates.

The **Goldcrest** *(Regulus regulus)* is a tiny bird normally abundant in the moorland conifer plantations. It prefers these trees, particularly in the breeding season, but also occurs in mixed woodland. Its numbers tend to be reduced in severe winters.

The **Whinchat** *(Saxicola rubetra)*, a summer visitor, is found on commons and moorland, Dartmoor being one of its most-favoured Devonshire localities. It feeds on insects and their larvae, and other small invertebrates.

The **Curlew** *(Numenius arquata)*, a large wader with a distinctive curved bill and a liquid bubbling call, occurs on the moors in the breeding season, after which it descends to the estuaries and lowland marshes. Its diet consists of many kinds of animal material, mainly invertebrate (but small frogs have been recorded), also the berries and seeds of moorland plants.

The **Snipe** *(Gallinago gallinago)* in Devon breeds mainly on wet moorland, particularly on Dartmoor. It feeds on invertebrates, including insects and their larvae, molluscs, and especially worms; also grass and various seeds.

The **Meadow Pipit** *(Anthus pratensis)* is abundant on Dartmoor in summer, where it breeds in open country, its range including the highest moors, to the exclusion of most other small birds. Its food consists mainly of insects and their larvae, and other small invertebrates. It tends to forsake the moors in winter.

The **Cuckoo** *(Cuculus canorus)* is well-suited to spending breeding seasons on the moor, where Meadow Pipits' nests are plentiful; it feeds on a wide range of invertebrates, including the hairy larvae rejected by most other birds.

Other species include the following breeding birds; they occur at widely differing population levels, and most of them shun the higher moors.

Mallard	Blackbird	Magpie
Sparrow Hawk	Song Thrush	Jackdaw
Pheasant	Mistle Thrush	Rook
Woodpigeon	Garden Warbler	Carrion Crow
Tawny Owl	Blackcap	Starling
Green Woodpecker	Chiffchaff	House Sparrow
Great Spotted Woodpecker	Willow Warbler	Greenfinch
Swallow	Spotted Flycatcher	Goldfinch
House Martin	Long-tailed Tit	Siskin
Pied Wagtail	Marsh Tit	Linnet
Wren	Coal Tit	Redpoll
Dunnock	Great Tit	Crossbill
Robin	Tree Creeper	Bullfinch
	Jay	Yellowhammer

There are some additional breeding species, particularly around the fringe (see Sitters, 1988), and of course the passage migrants, winter visitors and other non-breeding birds.

This is not the place to discuss rarities, but there are a couple which I can't resist mentioning, both cranes, of unexplained origin - a Demoiselle which I photographed at the Bala Brook water treatment works in 1971, and a Sarus which turned up at Bellever forestry houses round about that time.

Fishes

River Lamprey *(Lampetra fluviatilis)*
Salmon *(Salmo salar)*
Brown Trout *(S. trutta)*
Grayling *(Thymallus thymallus)*

Minnow *(Phoxinus phoxinus)*
Loach *(Nemacheilus barbatula)*
Common Eel *(Anguilla anguilla)*
Three-spined Stickleback
(Gasterosteus aculeatus)

Other Vertebrates

The **Common** or **Viviparous Lizard** *(Lacerta vivipara).*
Of the six species of British reptiles, four occur on
Dartmoor. This species is one of the moor's
characteristic vertebrates.

Few other vertebrates may advertise their presence, but now and again
one comes across representatives of less familiar groups. We can
expect occasionally to spot a Common Lizard, or perhaps a basking
Adder. Prof. Harvey (in the New Naturalist *Dartmoor*) listed eight
species of fishes (see above), the Common Frog, the Toad and Palmate
Newt; and in addition to the reptiles I have mentioned, the Grass-snake
and Slow-worm occur less frequently.

Adder

Invertebrates

Apart from the ubiquitous **Black Slug** *(Arion ater)* which, with others of its shell-less tribe, represents the Mollusca here, where shell-forming calcareous material is rare, the most familiar members of the invertebrate fauna in open country are probably the Lepidoptera associated with heathland vegetation. These include the Fox Moth and the Emperor, large day-flying moths which are often seen in rapid flight over the moors, and their larvae are encountered in the ground cover. (I have found the longitudinally-striped larva of the Broom Moth as common as any on Heather and Bracken.) Little Grass-moths are in evidence at the appropriate time of year, as are other small heathland moths; and it is not unusual to see familiar "garden" butterflies augmenting the residents - I have seen a Red Admiral at Two Bridges as late as November.

Among the Coleoptera, Bumble-dors or Dung-beetles are common; Dartmoor is an ideal habitat. The Cleg, a "biting-fly", one of Dartmoor's less agreeable insects, is a Dipteron which in high summer settles upon one's person with no sign of warning, and draws blood with its sharp beak-like proboscis. Other flies which tend to be a nuisance are the swarms of smaller fry which frequent the edges of the forestry plantations.

Whilst the indigenous woodlands, with their high proportion of oak, support a rich insect population, the many fast-flowing streams and the abundant static water provide habitats for many species whose life-styles tie them to these particular kinds of environment. The "Neuropterous" orders, such as the Mayflies, Caddises and Stoneflies are well-represented, and several species of Dragonfly occur. The commonest of the latter on the high moors are the Black Darter and the Keeled Skimmer, but special mention goes to the beautiful *Calopteryx* Damselflies so frequently seen by the upland streams.

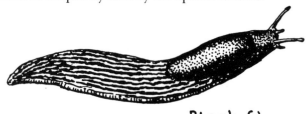

Black Slug

Some insects of moors and streams *(illustrated overleaf)*

The **Small Heath Butterfly** *(Coenonympha pamphilus)*, one of the smaller diurnal Lepidoptera to be seen on the open moor and in other grassy places.

The **Emperor Moth** *(Saturnia pavonia)*. The female, depicted here, flies at night, but may be seen in daylight in ground cover. The males fly rapidly across the moors in sunlight. The larvae, green with spotted black bands, pupate in silken cocoons which they spin among the herbage.

A **Grass-moth,** one of those small insects familiarly known as "crambites" (from their scientific family name) which are often disturbed as we walk through the grass, and which soon re-settle to lie along the stems with their wings folded tightly around their bodies.

The **Fox Moth** *(Macrothylacia rubi)* - the female is shown here - is another species of which the male is active in daylight, being the commonest large moth to be seen on moorland, where the food-plants of the hairy caterpillar include the three common heathers and whortleberry.

A **Mayfly** (Order Ephemeroptera). Mayflies are mostly quite small, and are interesting in that, having lived as aquatic nymphs for up to three years, they pass through a preliminary winged state (the sub-imago or "dun") before reaching the ephemeral fully adult stage (the "spinner"). They fall easy prey to trout, not only as rising nymphs, but also as sluggish duns, and as spent spinners after they have swarmed to mate and have descended to the surface. (Whilst often used by the entomologist in reference to the whole order, the term "Mayfly" is reserved by the angler for the genus Ephemera.)

A **Caddis-fly** (Order Trichoptera). These insects, which superficially resemble moths, have a coating of hairs on their wings instead of scales and, typically, chewing mouth-parts. Their larvae are generally aquatic, many of them living in cases constructed from a variety of materials (the material employed and the shape of the case being features often used in the determination of species).

A **Stonefly** (Order Plecoptera). These sluggish insects tend to hide in the vegetation by the fast-flowing streams in which their nymphs

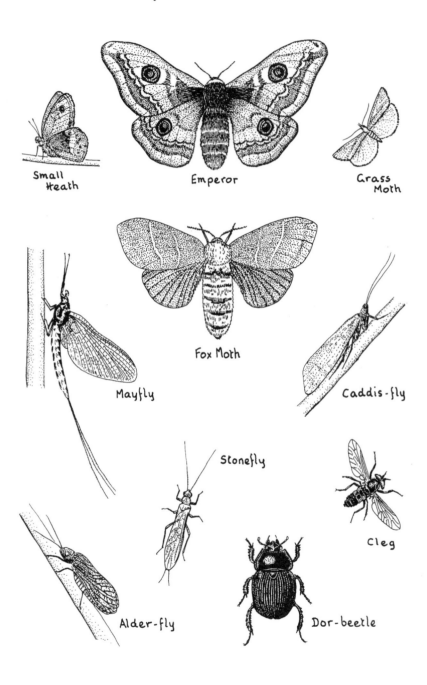

Small
Heath

Emperor

Grass
Moth

Fox Moth

Mayfly

Caddis-fly

Stonefly

Cleg

Alder-fly

Dor-beetle

small brown Willow Fly, however, a Stonefly common on Dartmoor, folds its wings cylindrically around its abdomen.

The **Cleg,** a grey dusty-looking two-winged fly, the female of which is a silent, sneaky attacker, folds its wings roof-wise over its back when at rest (or when helping itself to its victim's blood).

An **Alder-fly** (Order Megaloptera). The short-winged, primitive and clumsy adults do not venture far from the water in which they lived as larvae for a year. There are two British species.

The **Dung-beetle** or **Bumble-dor**, a very characteristic Dartmoor insect, is frequently met with; and its shards are often to be seen, having been rejected or voided by its predators.

Dragonflies and Damselflies *(illustrated overleaf)*

The **Golden-ringed Dragonfly** *(Cordulegaster boltonii)*, a "hawker" which is easily recognised by its colour-pattern of conspicuous yellow bands on a black background. It is a western and northern insect, with a flight period from the end of May until mid-September.

The **Common Darter** *(Sympetrum striolatum)* is yellow-brown, or red and yellow-brown. It is very skittish, returning frequently to rest on the same spot, often on a stone or bare ground. It is a late flier, being on the wing from mid-June until the end of October.

The **Common Blue Damselfly** *(Enallagma cyathigerum)* is one of the three species of blue damselfly most commonly encountered in the south-west. It flies from mid-May to early October. The Large Red Damselfly (Pyrrhosoma nymphula) is also on the Dartmoor list.

The **Broad-bodied Chaser** *(Libellula depressa)*. In view of the breadth of its body it is not difficult to distinguish this species from its near relatives. The colour of the abdomen is tawny brown in young individuals of both sexes and adult females, the males changing to powder blue as they mature. In all specimens there are yellow markings along the edges of the abdomen. The males are very territorial and aggressive towards other males.

The **Beautiful Demoiselle** *(Calopteryx virgo)*. The males of the two species of *Calopteryx* (once *Agrion*) have blue bodies and dark brown wing patches reflecting blue; the male Banded Demoiselle (C. splendens) has narrower wing patches. The females have green bodies with yellow or greenish transparent wings. *C.virgo*, which favours fast-running clear stony streams, is the species most likely to be seen on Dartmoor.

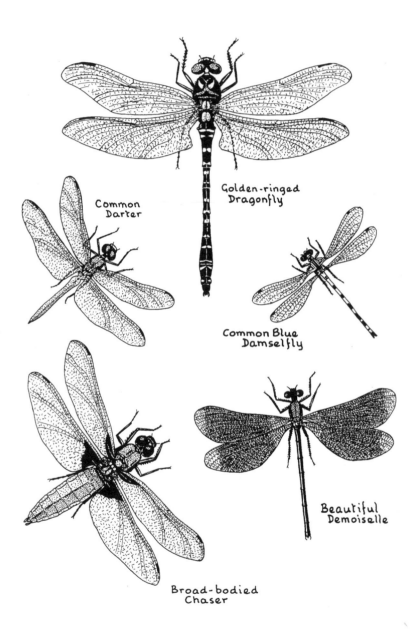

Golden-ringed
Dragonfly

Common
Darter

Common Blue
Damselfly

Broad-bodied
Chaser

Beautiful
Demoiselle

Dragonfly larvae

(a) **The Large Red Damselfly** *(Pyrrhosoma nymphula)*, a common and widespread species which lives in slow-moving or static water.

(b) The **Southern Hawker** *(Aeshna cyanea)* lives on the muddy floors of pools, the adults being more suited to the congenial habitats of the countryside around the moors.

(c) The **Broad-bodied Chaser** *(Libellula depressa)* also lives in the mud in static water.

(d) The **Black Darter** *(Sympetrum danae)* is a frequenter of peat-bogs, particularly in heathery areas. The body and legs of the mature male are completely black.

The **Keeled Skimmer** *(Orthetrum coerulescens)*. which breeds in *Sphagnum* bogs, is a small and slender insect. The abdomen of the adult male is powder-blue, that of the female and young male is yellow-brown.

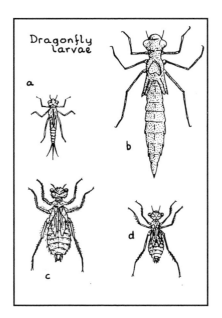

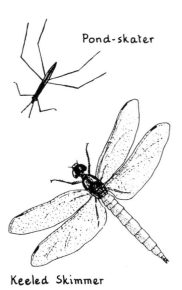

Keeled Skimmer

A **Pond-skater** *(Gerris najas)* . Active groups of this large species of water-bug (Hemiptera-Heteroptera) are often seen on the surface of little sheltered inlets along the margins of streams.

Livestock

The open moorland continues to serve its traditional purpose of providing rough grazing. As we have seen, certain nutrient deficiencies in the topsoil contribute to the growth of a range of characteristic plant species. Among them are plants (e.g. Bog Asphodel and Lousewort), which although merely indicators of poor grazing were once held responsible for a multitude of ailments in livestock. Some breeds are better able than others to cope with inferior feed, which accounts to a large extent for the kinds of animals favoured by the hill-farmer.

Dartmoor is primarily sheep country, and the **Scotch Blackface**, introduced early in the present century, and particularly suited to this environment, is widely distributed. The Exmoor Horn is a common breed, and others such as the **Cheviot** and various crosses are seen occasionally. However, neither the old White-faced Dartmoor, the true local breed, nor the improved Grey-faced are any longer much in evidence.

Among the beef cattle depastured on the high moor the commonest breed is the **Galloway** (usually black, sometimed belted, or dun). There is an admixture of other types, principally Aberdeen Angus; and the long-haired, long-horned **Highland** cattle are seen occasionally. The trend with the red South Devon cattle, one of the popular breeds nurtured on better grassland nearer home, is towards a dual-purpose beast, and in the in-country in recent years some newly-popular continental breeds have appeared.

Dartmoor has its own breed of **pony**, a small, hardy, intelligent animal which has the ability to thrive under extremely adverse conditions. However, for some considerable time one of the surest ways of seeing them was to visit a stud or agricultural show.

Piebalds and skewbalds, which are popular for riding, are excluded from the breed standards of the true Dartmoor - they may be any other conventional equine colour, preferably bay, black or brown.

The majority of the free-ranging stock has been of mixed blood, especially Shetland crosses, which lack the hardiness of the Dartmoor. Speculation as to their welfare and the ultimate fate of many of them has caused a great deal of concern among animal lovers.

In the forty years between 1949 and 1989 the number of ponies on the moor fell from 50,000 to 2,500.

Black Galloway and Highland cattle

Dartmoor Pony and Belted Galloways

Border Collie

Cheviot

Scotch Blackface

Two schemes were initiated in 1988, in an attempt to improve the hardiness and appearance of the ponies on the commons, the aim being to produce a type resembling the traditional Dartmoor.

The farmer's dog, in general terms, is the **Border Collie** which, though only comparatively recently admitted by the Kennel Club, has long been established as a sheep-dog.

A question often asked relates to the use of discretion when crossing a field in which there is a bull. There is a distinction here between dairy bulls and those of other breeds, and it is the responsibility of the farmer not to allow any dairy bull over the age of ten months free range of any field through which a path or bridleway passes. Bulls of other breeds must be accompanied by cows or heifers.

Part III

DARTMOOR BC - EARLY AD

Prehistoric Sites

The people of the Old Stone Age (Palaeolithic) were, it is believed, cave-dwelling hunters and food-gatherers - and their numbers must have been few, if only in view of the comparative scarcity of caves. (Kent's Cavern, well beyond the fringes of the moor, is a well-known Palaeolithic site). There is no evidence of Old Stone Age occupation of Dartmoor, although in 1931 a flint handaxe of Palaeolithic type was found on Brent Moor by R.Hansford Worth.

The Middle Stone Age people (Mesolithic, ca.8000-2500 BC) were probably nomadic hunters and food-gatherers, no longer essentially cave-dwelling. It could be said that the industrial archaeology of Dartmoor began with the manufacture of Mesolithic microliths. These tiny arrow-heads, spear-heads and tools of flint and chert (not occurring naturally in the area) have been found at several sites on the eastern side of the moor, and the hundreds of flint scraps found near the site of Fernworthy Reservoir indicate that manufacture took place on the spot, probably as a kind of itinerant industry.

The relics some of which perhaps symbolise prehistoric religious beliefs and rituals, beginning with those of the New Stone Age (Neolithic, ca.2500-2000 BC), are more frequent on the ground than in any other region in England - largely because of the abundance and durability of that material which has been used here for every conceivable application - the local stone.

Just as we have no proven understanding of the purpose of stone rows, "ceremonial" circles and menhirs, it would be a mistake to be too dogmatic about the age of prehistoric remains. I have tended to follow the convention of placing them in neat chronological compartments. However, there is no evidence that stone rows, for example, were entirely of the Beaker Period (see page 91) - they may have originated in the Neolithic. There is a possibility that the stones in these rows may have been preceded by wooden posts. There is, moreover, no guarantee that stone rows, or indeed complex "sanctuaries" were built up as entities - they may well have been modified and extended over a period of time.

The Neolithic Period

The New Stone Age people were the first farmers; they grew crops and reared livestock. Neolithic camps have been found off the moor, and the site of a hut of typical wattle-and-daub construction has been excavated at nearby Haldon. There is no real evidence of Neolithic settlement on Dartmoor, but some tools and arrow-heads have been found, and an investigation into a site near South Teign Head (and marked on some maps as a pound - at 640828) revealed that it possesses features commensurate with a Neolithic henge (Turner, 1984).

A basic diagnostic feature of a henge is a circular embankment with an internal ditch - thought to have had some religious significance in deterring encroachment by evil powers. (The much later Iron Age hillforts, very much larger than most henges, have ditches outside the banks.)

Unfortunately we know far too little about the way of life of the Neolithic people, and we have to turn to their burial sites to give us an indication that their association with Dartmoor was related to the country not far within its fringe.

A Neolithic site may show evidence of a long barrow with, at one end, a stone chamber in which multiple or successive interments are thought to have taken place - evidence from elsewhere suggests that this was certainly so.

There are the remains of several chamber tombs in Devon - most of those discovered are within the National Park - including some which suggest a transition to a round barrow design. Indeed, some of our large round barrows may well be of Neolithic date.

The Dartmoor prehistoric graves are typically in a dilapidated condition, their remains illustrating various elements of the original fabric. A chamber tomb which remains standing after its barrow has been destroyed is a "dolmen" (elsewhere a "cromlech" or "quoit"). I have included illustrations (see page 90) of the three examples mentioned by Worth, of which only one, Spinsters' Rock, is a recognisable dolmen. Since Worth wrote, evidence of more chamber tombs has come to light - one on Butterdon Hill (a long barrow at 660568, Ugborough: Fletcher, Grinsell and Quinnell in ProcDAS 32, 1974) and two in Gidleigh parish (simple tombs on the east slope of Buttern Hill at 659889 and 656885: J.R.Turner in ProcDAS 38, 1980).

Hemery (1983a) recorded the scant remains of a dolmen and a barrow south of the hollow of Piles Brook Head. He also mentioned and illustrated a dolmen "previously noted only by Rowe" (1896). I think Rowe was referring to the "Three Boys" which can only be regarded as a "possible" - only one stone remains.

Pearce (1981) and Grinsell (1978) include in their reviews of chamber tombs a structure near Meacombe with a massive capstone - I have followed Worth in including this under the heading of "kistvaens". Among the other objects which have been considered, at one time or another, to be dolmens, are the Judge's Chair in Dunnabridge Pound (very unlikely), a circular stone at Merrivale (an abandoned edge-runner) and a rock formation on Hawks Tor.

———————————— ◆ ————————————

(illustrated overleaf)
Spinsters' Rock (Drewsteignton, 700908), a reconstructed dolmen, in a field at Shilstone Farm, which represents the remains of a burial chamber; there is now no sign of a barrow.

Brent Fore Hill (South Brent, 669613). A dilapidated burial chamber with the remains of a long barrow, near Ball Gate (in the saddle between Brent Fore Hill and Corringdon Ball).

Cuckoo Ball (Ugborough, 659582). A ruined dolmen with a much reduced long barrow, 200 yards SSW of Cuckoo Ball Corner (i.e. near the wall that runs NNW from West Peeke, and within the angle at its most westerly point).

Spinsters Rock

Brent Fore Hill

Cuckoo Ball

The Beaker Period and Bronze Age

This period can be said to have begun about 2000 BC with the emergence of the Beaker culture - so named after a characteristic design of pottery. The Beaker people were herders and hunters, who knew the use of copper and bronze. They left no sign of settlement on the moor, but their sepulchral and "ritual" sites (small round barrows, stone rows, standing stones and "sanctuaries") are common.

From about the middle of the second millennium BC a firm occupation of the moor is thought to have taken place; this period is illustrated by the very many remains of stone enclosures (of irregular or roughly circular shape) and hut circles. Among the tumuli are some very large cairns of stone, which may be attributable to this later stage, but this is not certain - and this can also be said about their purpose. (I have heard it said that they may have been boundary markers.)

The Beaker and Bronze Age relics (often grouped together as Bronze Age) form a very numerous and widespread class of antiquities on the moor. Some of the dwellings and enclosures of the period were doubtless utilised by Iron Age people (who may also have made barrows), and by later settlers and itinerant workers.

There are numerous low earth-and-stone banks which it is assumed represent early land divisions, many of them having been generally accepted as medieval field systems. However, Elizabeth Gawne and J.V.Somers Cocks (TDA 100, 1968) recognised extensive patterns of low, long, parallel banks or "reaves" as prehistoric in origin. From a distance they can best be seen when the sun is low. Excavations on Holne Moor, carried out by Andrew Fleming, have revealed earlier boundary works underlying existing reaves, taking us back to a period of land division originating about 1600 BC. The mystery behind the adoption of this particular kind of boundary pattern remains unsolved. (See Fleming, 1968.)

Round barrows, cists and retaining circles

Although they are typically in a very disturbed condition it seems plain that few of the very numerous round barrows were constructed with the refinements of the concentric banks and ditches of the sophisticated Wessex barrows. Discounting the large stone cairns (where no clues to possible interment have been found) the Dartmoor round barrow is a mound of earth built up over a stone core. It seems to have been generally of an inverted bowl-shape, occasionally flat-topped. It was erected over a cist (or "kistvaen") or over an interment pit, or perhaps both, or occasionally on the site of a cremation. It was, in many cases, held in place by a circle of "set" stones. There are also uncommon "ring barrows", which consist of a circular bank, sometimes stone-faced, surrounding a flat central area. It has been seen that sometimes careful preparation of the site took place, including a certain amount of digging out.

Most of the barrows were opened before the advent of our present more enlightened approach to investigation, in the hope of finding something of immediate pecuniary value. Any old potsherds unearthed and discarded might have been treasure indeed, by today's archaeological standards. However, since the adoption of a more reasoned procedure, there have been records of a number of finds. Among them are fragments of pottery (several urns of various designs have been restored, charcoal, wood-ash, burnt bone, and artefacts such as flint knives and scrapers. A classic discovery was the amber pommel of a dagger, decorated with gold pins, from Two Barrows on Hameldon (and subsequently destroyed in an air-raid on Plymouth). The blade found here was one of the few bronze artefacts discovered on the moor. Another notable find was an archer's bracer of slate, found in a cist in Archerton Newtake (Forest, 636794).

Usually a cist was constructed with the end stones holding the side stones apart, but as the slabs were not too carefully selected a great deal of variation occurs in design. Rectangles are not necessarily regular, and occasionally a stone projects beyond the end of the structure, or very rarely two stones were used to form a side. Diversity in the present condition of cists is illustrated by many incomplete examples (such as those at White Tor and on Beacon Plain) and too generous restorations (e.g. at Roundy Park, at Merivale, and one of those on Lakehead Hill).

Though the Dartmoor cists are normally large enough to have contained crouched burials there is no certain evidence to support ideas of this form of interment. Beaker period crouched burials have been found at other sites in the West Country, but such interments would not have survived the acid Dartmoor soil. However, it seems to be accepted that the earlier (Beaker Period) burials were carried out by means of inhumation, and that the later (Bronze Age) remains were cremated.

Worth found that the Dartmoor kistvaens were orientated, with few exceptions, within the NW and SE quadrants. He compared these directions with the setting of the sun, and came to the conclusion that there seemed to be no connection. It occurred to me, on reading this, that if one considers not the longer, but the shorter axis, related to the direction in which a crouched burial might face, a relationship with the setting sun does now present itself. This seems credible in view of the considerable influence the sun must have had over the lives of these people. I see that Robert Burnard (1891) touched upon this idea when describing the "Bellaford Kistvaen". In view of the complete dearth of bodies facing either SW or NE this cannot be proved or disproved, but evidence from outside the area, again, might impart an inference for the Dartmoor cists. This is my only concession to astronomical inter-pretations applied to the orientation of the Dartmoor "ritual" sites. I have heard these theories disputed on the grounds that tree cover would confuse the issue, but I have an open mind on that aspect of the subject. (See Brian Byng.)

Cists are found with or without the remains of the cairn-retaining circle, and there are cairn circles with little or nothing within them to indicate what they may have enclosed. Some cairn circles are "open", i.e. with the stones relatively spaced out. In these circles the stones, in general, have no special characteristics, but there are exceptions in which they are tall and pillar-like, or in which they lean outwards. There are also "closed" retaining circles, in which the stones are contiguous.

A few multiple circles are known - for example, the Yar Tor double circle, four-fold circles near Yellowmead (Sheepstor) and on Shovel Down, and two arrangements, each with a probable minimum of six rings, at Glasscombe, Ugborough (ProcDAS 1981), adjacent to the multiple rows detailed by Worth and others. Discoveries by Rosemary Robinson and Judith Cosford (ProcDAS 1986) brought the total number of known Dartmoor multiple circles up to ten.

J.R.Turner (1990) has given a detailed analysis of the circular burial and ritual monuments, in which the sites are divided into seven categories (mostly with sub-divisions): stone rings, embanked stone circles, double kerb circles, ring settings, platform circles, encircled cairns and stone circles. (I have separated the last of these as "stone circles or sanctuaries".)

Barrows

An earth-and-stone barrow. This barrow, on Piles Hill (Harford, 653608) has been considerably disturbed (as is usual), and in such cases evidence of investigation is usually afforded by the presence of a central concavity. The barrow is unusual, however, in its similarity to bell-barrows of Wessex type - it stands on a platform of greater diameter than the mound, and surrounding the platform is a possible low bank.

Huntingdon Barrow (Forest, 662669). The usual situation for stone cairns is on hill-tops where they can be seen from a considerable distance, sometimes in groups or "barrow cemeteries". The cairn on the summit of Huntingdon Hill, otherwise known as the "Heap o' Sinners", is an isolated example which, like most others, has been much disturbed over the years.

Stalldon Barrow (Cornwood, 626623) lies east of the impressive stone row on Stall Moor. A small building, known as Hillson's House, was erected on it many years ago, and it has been related that a clock-maker lived there.

Eastern Whittaburrow (South Brent, 665651), an immense cairn on a ridge a mile to the west of the Avon Dam, when measured by Crossing was found to be "90 yards in circumference and 12 yards in height". The grotesque reshaping, which makes it easily recognisable from a distance, is relatively modern, but the reason for it is not clear.

Barrow on Piles Hill

Huntingdon Barrow

Skalldon Barrow

Eastern Whitaburrow

Drizzlecombe

Merrivale

Legis Lake

Drewston

Langcombe

Thornworthy

Cists (I)

Drizzlecombe (Sheepstor, 591672). A good example of a cist, complete with cover-stone (dislodged as usual), situated on a hillside particularly rich in prehistoric relics.

Merivale (Walkhampton, 555747). The kistvaen, near the stone rows on Long Ash Hill, was said by Worth to have been too generously restored after it had been damaged in the mid-19th century - two gateposts had been cut from the cover-stone.

Legis Lake (Sheepstor, 566657). This cist is 500 yards to the WNW of Legis Tor, and loosely associated with other relics in this part of Ringmoor Down.

Drewston (Chagford, 725869). A structure in a field near Meacombe - a massive cover-stone on two supporters, now classified as a chamber tomb.

Langcombe (Shaugh Prior, 605671). A cist near Plym Steps, one of several in the valley of Langcombe Brook.

Thornworthy (Chagford, 667843). The site is near the north bank of Fernworthy Reservoir, 300 yards west of the dam. A smaller cist, now in Torquay Museum, was found in the same barrow.

Cists (II) *(illustrated overleaf)*

Blakey Tor (Forest, 613735). Above the right bank of Blackabrook, and a short distance south of the tor.

White Tor (Peter Tavy, 547787). Between the tor and Langstone Moor menhir, the scanty remains of a cist constructed from the local greenstone.

Roundy Park (Forest, 639797). Near the East Dart 1200 yards NW of Postbridge, a massive chamber with two cover-stones, thought to be a lavish restoration.

Beacon Plain (Ugborough, 658593). 350 yards approx. east of Hanger-shell Rock. The only signs of a burial site are three stones of a kistvaen.

Lakehead Hill (Forest, 642777). At the edge of the clearing in Bellever Plantation, 400 yards SSW of Krapps Ring.

Joan Ford's Newtake (Forest, 631721). Within the enclosure wall 300 yards NNW of the Swincombe water intake.

White Tor

Blakey Tor

Roundy Park

Beacon Plain

Lakehead Hill

Joan Ford's
Newtake

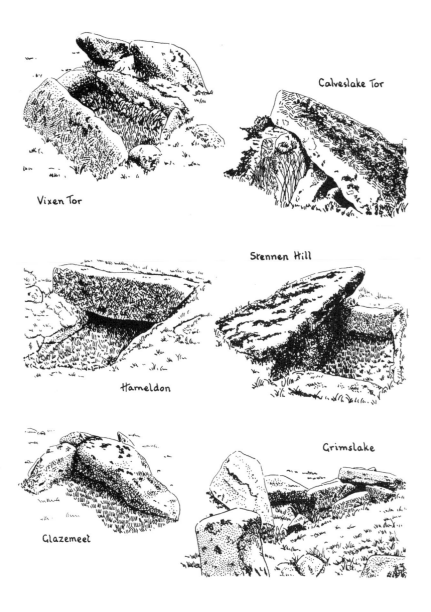

Vixen Tor

Calveslake Tor

Hameldon

Stennen Hill

Glazemeet

Grimslake

Cists (III) *(illustrated on previous page)*

Vixen Tor (Whitchurch, 542743), between the tor and the enclosure wall to the north.

Calveslake Tor (Shaugh Prior, 609676), south of the head of Calveslake, a small tributary of the Plym.

Hameldon (Widecombe, 710784), 600 yards SSE of Hameldon Beacon.

Stennen Hill (Forest, 625779), above the right bank of Cherry Brook 500 yards NNW of the Powder Mills. There is another, very ruined cist 90 yards SSE.

Glazemeet (Ugborough, 667605). Very little is left of this cist which lies above West Glaze Brook, between Glazemeet and Glasscombe Corner.

Grimslake (North Bovey, 704811), about 400 yards ENE of Grimspound, and 100 yards north of the head of the stream.

Cists with retaining circles

Royal Hill (Forest). South-east of the summit of Royal Hill there is a series of three denuded barrows, each visible from the next. The two illustrated (north 621724, and south 620721) have dilapidated kistvaens. The central barrow has a good cist, as has the "Crock of Gold", approx. 1200 yards to the north-west. Other relics in the area include Brockenborough (a barrow on the hill to the south-west of the southern cairn-circle) and cists at Blakey Tor and in Joan Ford's Newtake (see page 97).

Grimsgrave (Shaugh Prior, 612664), one of a number of graves in Langcombe, illustrating a variation in design, in which the stones of the retaining circle lean outwards.

Hound Tor (Manaton, 741788). Midway between the tor and the road to the south-west, there is a retaining circle of stones set without spaces between them, a design which Worth called "closed" retaining circles, as opposed to the more widely-spaced (and more usual) "open" arrangement.

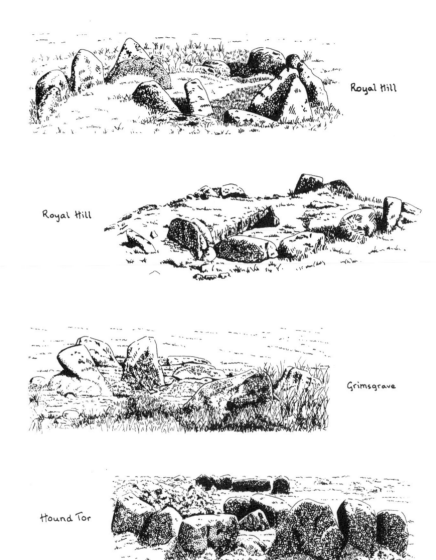

Royal Hill

Royal Hill

Grimsgrave

Hound Tor

Cosdon

A double kistvaen in the barrow at the end of the Cosdon triple stone row (South Tawton, 643916), a unique occurrence where two cists share a common end-stone. (The two cists at Thornworthy were separate.)

Yellowmead

The four-fold circle on **Yellowmead Down** (Sheepstor, 574678) has a diameter of 65 feet - more than double the size of the Shovel Down four-fold circle (30 feet). There are some groups of stones nearby which indicate that there was an associated double row. Grinsell's review (1978) contains a good aerial photograph of this circle, and Tom Greeves included another in his collection of illustrations (1985).

Stone rows

There are over sixty known stone rows on Dartmoor. Most of them are either single or double (sometimes a combination of both) and there are various examples of multiple rows. A typical stone row may be terminated at one end by a cairn or the remains of one such as a retaining circle (suggesting a ritual significance) and at the other end by a blocking-stone (i.e. a flattish stone set at right angles to the direction of the row). A frequent feature is an increase in the size of the stones as they approach the site of the barrow.

From short, "suspected" rows of small, possibly "set" stones, they increase in certainty, in length and/or size of individual members. The longest row runs northward from the retaining circle on Stall Moor (the Dancers) to a barrow on Green Hill, a distance of over 2 miles. The Stalldon row, more than a mile to the south, is the most impressive in respect of the size of stones.

There are numerous small stones above the right bank of the East Glaze (a few yards north of the wall between Ball Gate and Glasscombe Corner) which seem to represent seven, or possibly eight, parallel rows, and a separate row of larger stones nearby. There are associated cairns and multiple stone circles (Robinson, Griffiths and Cosford, 1990).

◆

(illustrated overleaf)

Hurston Ridge (Chagford, 672825). On Chagford Common, a mile to the north of the Warren House Inn, there is a double row terminated at one end by a cairn and at the other by a blocking-stone.

On **Challacombe Down** (North Bovey, 690808) there is a good example of a triple stone row (reconstructed), although it has been shortened at one end by mining operations.

Merrivale (Walkhampton, 554748). On Long Ash Hill, ESE of Merrivale Bridge, there are two parallel double rows. A barrow interrupts one of them at the centre. In close proximity there is a massive kistvaen and other barrows. From one of the latter runs an insignificant single row. Nearby there are two menhirs and a "sanctuary" circle .

Hurston Ridge

Challacombe

Merrivale

Hingston Hill

Shovel Down

Stalldon

(illustrated on previous page)
Hingston Hill (Walkhampton, 588693). Often referred to as the Down Tor row, this alignment runs from a retaining circle which stands 650 yards ESE of the tor, and terminates 200 yards short of a cairn in the same line, ENE. The stones nearest the retaining circle, particularly the one adjacent to it, are large in comparison with the others.

Shovel (Shuffle, Shuggle) Down (Chagford, 659860). There is a complex arrangement here, of which the three double rows depicted comprise the northern section. Approximately where they meet there is a four-fold retaining circle. Associated with other rows to the south there is a menhir, the Longstone (adopted as a Forest boundary mark) and the "Three Boys", now only one stone, probably representing the larger stones which are frequently found near the end of a row (Worth).

Stalldon (Cornwood, 623632). This single row, 544 yards in length, stands on the hill known as Stalldon Barrow (the name rightfully applies to the cairn - 450 yards to the east of the row). The stones are very large and conspicuous (some of them being over 8 feet in height), rendering the row unique on Dartmoor.

◆

Complex ceremonial sites

In addition to the complex sites I have mentioned (Shovel Down and Merrivale) - I use the term "ceremonial" from supposition - there are others at Drizzlecombe (Sheepstor, 592670), where there are stone rows, menhirs and barrows (including a sizeble mound, the "Giant's Basin"), and on Froggymead Hill, Fernworthy (Forest, 655841), where there are stone rows, barrows and a "sanctuary" circle.

A general impression of the layout of these sites can be gained from the 1:25,000 map, and detailed plans are to be found in Worth (who suggested a planned symmetry at Drizzlecombe and Pettit (1974).

Menhirs

In some of the stone rows there are, as we have seen, comparatively tall stones which would attract particular attention if they were standing in isolation. There are some stones, in fact, which are sufficiently distinct in size or the manner of their siting to be placed in a special category. These are known as menhirs, or longstones. Like the stone rows and "sanctuaries" their purpose is not known - suffice it to say that they can be assumed to have had some ritual significance. The name "Longstone", which has been applied to various specific menhirs (especially those at Harbourne Head, on Piles Hill and on Shovel Down), is also to be seen in modified form in the name of the site of another menhir - Langstone Moor.

(illustrated overleaf)
The Longstone, Shovel Down (Chagford/Gidleigh/Forest, 660857). A squarish pillar, 10ft 5in. in height, an extension of the complex of remains 800 yards to the south-west of Castor Rock, it has been utilised as a boundary marker.

Drizzlecombe (Thrushelcombe) (Sheepstor). There are three menhirs here, one at the south-west end of each of the stone rows; they were re-erected in 1893. To distinquish between them I have used the letters applied by Worth. Menhir C (592670), a broad, flat slab with a peculiar but natural projection at the top, stands 60 yards north of the Giant's Basin barrow; at 14ft in height, it is the tallest megalith on Dartmoor.

Merivale (Walkhampton, 554746). The re-erected menhir on Long Ash Hill is 10ft 4in. in height. Its lower half is flat and broadly triangular, but in thickness it narrows towards the base. Its upper half is square in section, and tapers towards the top.

Langstone Moor (Peter Tavy, 550787), by the Lichway, 800 yards east of White Tor. Re-erected, it stands about 9ft in height, is fairly square in section, but has a marked "kink" in the middle. The stone is not of granite, as are the other menhirs, but of an epidiorite which occurs in this locality. It has been damaged by small arms fire. A row of small stones runs to the north for about 110 yards, with traces of a barrow at the far end.

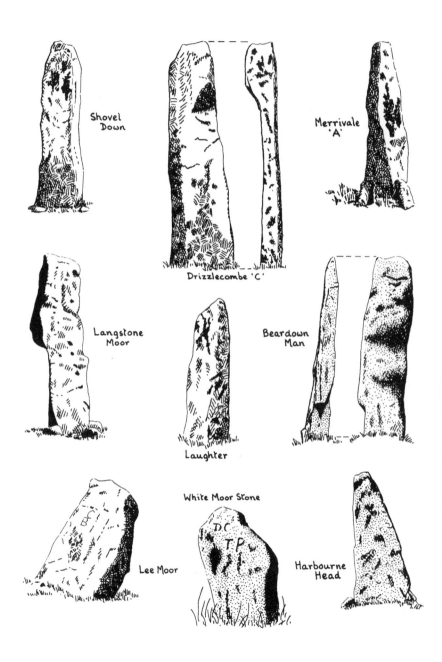

Shovel Down

Merrivale 'A'

Drizzlecombe 'C'

Langstone Moor

Beardown Man

Laughter

White Moor Stone

Lee Moor

Harbourne Head

Laughter Newtake (Forest, 652754), 300 yards south of Laughter Tor. This is a smooth and regular pillar, 8ft 8in. in height, of squarish section and with a sloping top. A stone row runs ESE towards the track between Dunnabridge Pound and Laughter Hole Farm.

Beardown Man (Forest, 595796) is an isolated broad flat slab, over 11ft in height, standing above the left bank of the Cowsic, not far from its source, and a short distance to the west of Devil's Tor.

The Hanging Stone or **Leaning Rock** (Shaugh Prior, 584637),1200 yards ENE of the Big Pond on Lee Moor, is 7ft 9in. in height, and of a fairly regular, squat, rectangular shape, but leaning considerably out of the vertical. There are letters inscribed upon it - Worth considered them to be CB (and it is not difficult to read them as such) whilst Hemery (1983a.) interpreted them as SP (for Shaugh Prior).

White Moor Stone (Forest/Throwleigh, 633895) is a broad, flat slab, 5ft 6in. in height, south-west of Raybarrow Pool, and 700 yards northeast of Hound Tor (the Little Hound Tor or Parva Hundetorre referred to in the ancient lists of Forest bondmarks, but Round Tor according to Hemery). The stone has been utilised as a boundary marker. There is a cairn 100 yards north-west, and the White Moor stone circle is 170 yards NNW.

The Longstone, Harbourne Head (Dean Prior, 697651), about 170 yards east of Harbourne Head, is an isolated slab about 8ft in height, broad and flat, with its broad aspect tapering strongly to the top.

Mardon Down (Moretonhampstead, 770878). A 6ft pillar known as the Maximajor Stone or Headless Cross - a possible menhir (not the remains of a cross). Destroyed by vandals in 1990, and replaced by a replica two years later.

Drizzlecombe. Menhirs A and B (10ft 6in. and 7ft 9in. in height) stand 180 yards south-west of the Giant's Basin. (590668 and 591670.)

The Longstone, Piles Hill (654607). 160 yards south-east of the cairn on the summit, the stone is the terminal member of the Butterdon stone row, which here marks the Harford/Ugborough boundary. 8ft 5in. long, it is of squarish section, tapering towards its apex, and has had a piece cut from it. The menhir, now re-erected, stands beside a later boundary post.

Beacon Plain (Ugborough, 659592). About 400 yards ESE of Hangershell Rock, two massive stones lie 57 yards apart in an otherwise generally stone-free area. One is a broad, flattish "whaleback" of a stone, and the other a more regular square-sectioned pillar. Worth thought they could be fallen menhirs.

Merrivale. This recumbent stone lies 35ft from the standing menhir and is comparatively insignificant, being only about 7ft.long.

Butterdon Hill
(Moretonhampstead, 748884). Brian le Messurier (1980) drew attention to an unmapped monolith alongside the foot- path that runs SSE from Cranbrook Farm, and opposite the summit of Butterdon Hill.

Butterdon Down

At least one other possible menhir has been recorded; in the Oxenham Arms at South Zeal (South Tawton, 651935) there is a massive pillar incorporated into an interior wall.

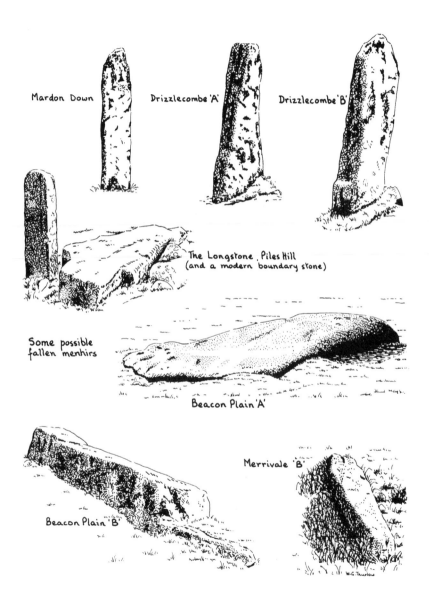

Mardon Down

Drizzlecombe 'A'

Drizzlecombe 'B'

The Longstone, Piles Hill
(and a modern boundary stone)

Some possible
fallen menhirs

Beacon Plain 'A'

Beacon Plain 'B'

Merrivale 'B'

Stone circles (or sanctuaries)

The term "stone circle" is one which has been applied to a specific class of antiquities in order to distinguish them from the circles associated with prehistoric dwellings and earth-and-stone barrows. They are larger than any of the hut circles, and the smallest of them (Merrivale) is marginally smaller that the largest cairn-retaining circle (Yellowmead Down).

They have not been shown to be associated with actual burials, but they may be assumed to have had some religious, or other ceremonial significance - there is evidence that fires were lit within them. Many of the stones have been re-erected, mostly during the Victorian period of feverish archaeological activity, and there are cases where it is suspected that during "restoration" some of the stones put up were not the originals. Most of the measurements I have given are those recorded by Worth.

───────────── ✦ ─────────────

Brisworthy (Sheepstor, 564655). A restored circle near the southern edge of Ringmoor Down, north of the wall of the Brisworthy enclosures. Dia.79ft.

Fernworthy (Forest, 655841). Part of a group of antiquities on Froggymead Hill, within Fernworthy Plantation. Dia.64ft 6in. The complex includes stone rows and barrows.

White (Whit) Moor (South Tawton, 633896). Dia.66ft. A circle with stones of varying size, south of the summit of Little Whit Hill (OS Little Hound Tor, but there is no tor - see Hemery, 1983a). Crossing's Track 41 (South Zeal to Hangingstone Hill) passes it on its west side. White Moor Stone is 170 yards SSE.

Merrivale (Walkhampton, 554746).Dia.62ft. Belongs to the group of relics on Long Ash Hill. Not only is the circle small in diameter by comparison with other circles of its class, but its stones are also of modest size.

Grey Wethers (Forest, 639831) . Two adjacent circles 600 yards N of E from Sittaford Tor. The stones are fairly substantial and are unusual in being generally flat-topped. Dia. north circle 103ft 6in. south circle 116ft 6in. (The Vitifer Mine leat passes to the north-east.)

Scorhill (Gidleigh, 654874). Dia.88ft. On Scorhill Down, 350 yards north of the confluence of the North Teign and Wallabrook. The stones are generally pointed and of moderate dimensions, but the circle is rendered impressive by the size of one of its members - about 8ft tall.

Langstone Moor (Peter Tavy, 556782). 800 yards south-east of the Langstone menhir and 600 yards above the right bank of the Walkham. There are several substantial stones standing, though considerable damage was done during the military occupation at the time of the second world war. Dia.67ft.

✦

Some circles not illustrated
Buttern Hill (Gidleigh, 649885). Dia.81ft. A very dilapidated circle, in the saddle between Buttern Hill and Kennon Hill.

Down Ridge (Forest, 655720). Dia.81ft. A fragment of a circle on the north slope of the ridge above the Hexworthy enclosures. The stones are large rectangular slabs.

Mardon Down (Moretonhampstead, 767872). Dia.24ft 6in. High on the western part of the down, 150 yards south of the track which crosses it from east to west. Rediscovered by L.V.Grinsell in 1972 (see ProcDAS 32, 1974). A ruinous circle of about 23 stones, of which two are standing and three are leaning; there are two other stones outside the circle to the south-west.

Sherberton (Forest, 639732). Dia.96ft. A dilapidated circle of small stones, on the ridge between the West Dart and its tributary the Swincombe, 700 yards WSW of Sherberton.

The Grey Wethers

North Circle

continued below

South Circle

Scorhill

Langstone Moor

Sourton (547895). Dia.110ft. A fallen circle, discovered in the mid-1900s, in the saddle between Sourton Tors and Corn Ridge, and ENE of the head of Deep Valley. (An abandoned apple-crusher lies nearby.)

Willings Walls Warren (Shaugh Prior, 582652). Dia.37ft 6in. Worth described an unusual setting of four clusters of stones midway between Hentor Brook and Spanish Lake, and a stone in a reave which crosses the east side of the site, marking a possible fifth point. The five points, thus positioned, could have marked the circumference of a circle, or the points of a fairly regular pentagon.

Prehistoric dwellings

The remains of prehistoric huts found on Dartmoor (about 4000 are known) are typically low circles of stones, i.e. the lowest course of a wall, often set in earthen banks. The original wall would itself have been low, and the roof is likely to have consisted of a conical arrangement of boughs, supported by uprights in the larger huts, and with a covering of turf and herbage or skins.

Some hut circles are not conspicuous because so little remains of the original structure, and there are many, such as some of those at Merrivale, which though quite substantial are not necessarily easy to pick out because they lie in heavily rock-strewn areas. There are huts in whose walls are massive blocks of stone, and diligent searching will find circles with door-jambs still in position.

It has been established in recent years that in some cases where a hut was built on a gradient the ground was raised on the lower side to level the floor.

In some huts there are signs of interior furnishings, such as sleeping platforms - the ultimate is reached in a "king-size" dais at Broadun (Forest, 635800); and at Ryders Rings (see page 117) excavation of a hut revealed a trigged-up stone fire shield. In this dwelling there were also cooking stones, charcoal, typical fragments of pottery, flint chips, and part of a red grit whetstone.

There are the remains of huts which show evidence of an entrance passage shielding the doorway (e.g. at Merrivale, 558747), and a few with designs slightly more pretentious, such as the one I have illustrated near Bala Brook (see page 119), and a hut at Foale's Arrishes with a small extension (Widecombe, 737758). The latter seems to have had Iron Age connections, as does a hut at the Kestor settlement (664868) where the circular wall is set within a small enclosure (the Round Pound) and connected to it by radiating partition walls. However, the probability of re-use and possible modification of some huts within historic times, say by tinners, should not be overlooked.

Many of the hut circles occur singly or in small groups; others are in larger groups representing close-knit settlements, some within enclosure walls. There may be a single hut within its own small enclosure, as for example at Tunhill Rocks (Widecombe, 732758), but it is more usual to find enclosures representing communal life. The design of the prehistoric enclosures described in the early years of Dartmoor exploration (i.e. those more easily recognised) extends to large and complex compounds, often circular or irregular in shape, some with many huts and stock pens. A well-known example is Ryders Rings (South Brent, 678643) where there are two contiguous enclosures of irregular shape with a number of hut circles within, and pens along the inner walls.

There are a dozen or so large unenclosed hut groups, for example those at Watern Oke (5683) and Standon Down (5582), both overlooking the Tavy. Some of the huts in these villages have connecting walls, providing compounds for stock.

With further knowledge of the moor's surface, gained by the application of modern techniques, it is seen that the patterns of parallel land division mentioned earlier have their associated hut circles.

In addition to the familiar stone huts, it is now known that there were wooden round houses, evidence of which is only detectable by excavation. (It is debatable whether the term "round house" should be too freely used in relation to prehistoric dwellings, as it has long been used for a type of post-medieval farm building which housed a stone mill for grinding or crushing apples, grain and furze.)

The 1:25000 map shows that the highest concentration of the more visible remains of prehistoric settlements occurs in the south and west, particularly in the vicinity of the main rivers. They are best seen when the bracken cover is minimal.

A prehistoric doorway - one of the huts with door-jambs still standing, at the settlement known as Standon Houses (Peter Tavy, 550824).

Hut entrance - Standon Down

Merrivale (Walkhampton, 555750). One of the numerous hut circles in this vicinity, representative of the condition of very many of the Dartmoor prehistoric dwellings.

Shapley Common (North Bovey, 694822). It is less usual to find a hut wall constructed of massive stones such as these. This hut is one of a group near the head of Curlicombe Brook, and visible from New Road 800 yards south of Challacombe Cross.

Bala Brook (South Brent, 672630). Harry Starkey (1981) drew attention to three huts among a group on the stream's left bank; each of them contains a comparatively minute chamber with a diminutive doorway - these may have been used for small animals or perhaps for storage.

Grimspound (Manaton, 701808). This hut was liberally restored many years ago, and features a well-defined doorway, sheltered by an entrance passage.

A typical
hut circle
- Merrivale

Massive stones
in a hut wall -
Shapley Common

A small chamber
within a hut -
Bala Brook

A restored
hut circle -
Grimspound

Hut circle - Butterbrook

Enclosure wall - Smallacombe Rocks

Grimspound - the main gateway

Butterbrook (Harford, 644593). One of several hut circles near the small reservoir south-east of Harford Moor Gate.

At **Smallacombe Rocks** (Ilsington, 756782) a prehistoric enclosure makes use of a natural rock-pile to form part of its wall.

Grimspound (Manaton/North Bovey), lying near the head of Grim's Lake between Hookner Tor and Hameldon, is the best-known of many enclosed hut groups; it contains twenty-four huts and some stock pens. (700808).

The Iron Age

The age of the Celts, or "ancient Britons" - the last prehistoric period - from about 500 BC, seems to have lasted on Dartmoor, in effect, into the Dark Ages, because of the low level of Roman influence in the region. The early Celts of "Iron Age A" were essentially farmers, and the remains of some of the huts they occupied (circles of stone of Bronze Age type) show a clear association with large groups of small rectangular fields.

There are major Iron Age open settlements at Foale's Arrishes (Widecombe, 738760) and at Kestor (Chagford, 665869).

Field boundaries, Kestor. This pastoral site to the north of Castor Rock (and now crossed by the road from Teigncombe to Batworthy) consists of an extensive pattern of rectangular fields with access lanes and hut circles.

Typical of the culture of the later invaders of "Iron Age B" (who introduced the horse to Britain, and perhaps, thus, the pony to Dartmoor) are "hill-forts" or encampments (large enclosures surrounded by substantial banks and ditches, and commonly called "castles"). There are about twenty hill-fort sites strategically placed around the moorland fringe. Those with a single bank and ditch are referred to as "univallate" (U/v in the following list), and those with multiple banks and ditches as "multivallate" (M/v). The best-known of them include three above the Teign Gorge:

Cranbrook Castle (Moretonhampstead, 738890), a site enclosing about 8 acres above a steep slope on the south bank of the river. (M/v.)

Prestonbury Castle (Drewsteignton, 747900), a 3 acre site high above the north bank of the Teign, overlooking Fingle Bridge. (M/v.)

Wooston Castle (Moretonhampstead, 765896), 6 acres in extent, lies on the south bank, downstream from Cranbrook and Prestonbury, from which it differs primarily in being overlooked by higher ground on one side; it was probably, therefore, less significant in a military context.

Other sites are:

Boro Wood Castle (Ashburton, 749716)
Brent Hill (South Brent, 704617) (M/v)
Brent Tor (Brentor, 471804) (M/v)
Dewerstone Camp (Meavy, 538640) (M/v)
Hembury Castle (Holne, 724684) (U/v)
Holne Chase Castle (Holne, 724719) (U/v)
Hunter's Tor (Lustleigh, 761824) (M/v)
Hound Tor Camp (Manaton, 768805) (U/v)
Okehampton Camp (O.Hamlets, 604941) (U/v)
Place Wood Camp, or Tower Hill Castle (Ashburton, 762714) (U/v)
White Tor (Peter Tavy, 542786) (M/v)

Apart from evidence of iron working, Dartmoor finds from this period include pottery, currency bars, and a single coin.

There are aerial views of the hill-forts at Brent Tor, Cranbrook and Prestonbury, and of the field system at Kestor, in Greeves, 1985.

Dartmoor AD

The Dark Ages

It is known that the Romans were active in certain areas around the moor - there are signs that one of their roads skirted its northern flank towards Cornwall. Evidence of a route on the south side is more tenuous, although a Roman road has long been claimed as far as Teign Bridge, and in the spring of 1993 a Roman site was unearthed at Penn Inn, Newton Abbot. There is a small earthwork which may have been a signalling station to the south of Okehampton church, and the site of a possible fortlet and road at Sourton Down (Pearce, 1981). More relevant to our subject is that a 2nd century Roman coin was recently discovered on the moor (DAS Newsletter, May 1988).

There is little other evidence, but associated with the transitional period between prehistoric and historic times - the Dark Ages - there are a number of relics known as Celtic memorial stones, on which there are inscriptions showing a distinct Roman influence over the local population around the moor.

Sourton Green

Incised stone on Sourton Green (543903). This pillar, thought to be an early Christian memorial, was erected here in the mid-1980s, having been moved from a nearby farm, where it had been used as a support for the roof of a shed.

Some Celtic Memorial Stones

Lustleigh Church

Sourton Down

Sticklepath

Sourton Cross. This inscribed pillar stood at 547917 (Sourton Down Crossroads), and was moved to a nearby position because of road-works. It is thought to have been cut into the shape of a cross subsequent to its original siting; this would account for its very short arms.

Stone in Lustleigh Church (785813). This stone is rather badly worn as a result of having been used as a threshold in the porch; it has been taken from that vulnerable position and now stands inside the church.

The inscribed pillar at Sticklepath (639941) stands where the road from Belstone joins the highway at the west end of the village.

✦

In addition to the Celtic memorial stones illustrated there are three collected together in a private garden in Tavistock (the Vicarage), and another, from Fardel near Ivybridge, in the British Museum.

The Saxons established settlements around the moor, and they would have used the high ground for pasture. Their widespread influence on Dartmoor is illustrated by the frequent occurrence of place-names ending in -cott and -worthy. There are several streams called Wallabrook, and the suggestion has been made that the Saxons were referring to the native Britons (i.e. "the brook of the Weala" - the Welsh or Celts).

The outline of a Saxon street plan has been identified at Lydford, which was one of four Devon mints, but the Dark Ages, although now less dark than hitherto, have left very little in the form of structural remains. Investigations of medieval sites have shown that many buildings of this later period replaced earlier wood-framed structures which the Saxons seemed to have preferred.

The Middle Ages

By the time of Domesday (1086) Lydford and Okehampton had been established as significant Norman sites, by the founding of a promontory fort at Lydford (the site is south-west of the church) and the castle at Okehampton. At Plympton a round keep survives on the site of the original castle, built and demolished in the 12th century. Though far removed from the present edge of the moor, Plympton is relevant as one of the four Stannary Towns. Gidleigh Castle, incidentally, a small building with cellar below and solar above, was a fortified manor house erected in about 1300.

The first farmsteads of this period were established (ca.1150-1250) in the more easily accessible valleys - some of these became known as "ancient tenements".

Life on Dartmoor has traditionally revolved around the production of wool, and the peaceful, pastoral scene which may well have prevailed was no doubt decidedly disturbed by the discovery of rich deposits of tin in south-west Dartmoor about the middle of the twelfth century, when the area was assailed by a rush of prospectors and settlers.

In recent years a number of early medieval sites have been investigated - the village between Hound Tor and Greator Rocks is a well-known example (Manaton, 746788). It is thought that such villages were abandoned probably about the time of the Black Death (1349) when a severe blow was dealt to a hitherto busy population. Although in numerous cases only low banks marking the sites of the buildings remain, many of the farmhouses which were constructed with substantial granite walls tended to survive, and some good examples can still be seen, often now serving as outhouses when they have been superseded by later, improved dwellings.

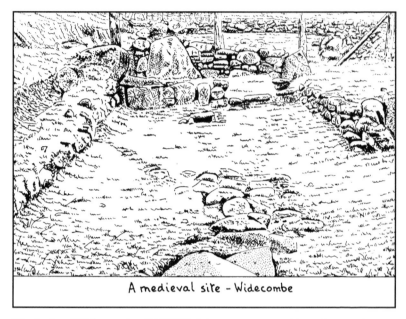

A medieval site - Widecombe

Hutholes (Widecombe, 703758). There are several huts here, where a process of individual rebuilding and expansion took place, detected by the position of the post-holes - the posts having formed the basic fabric of the wattle-and-daub buildings - and the low stone walls marking the later, more permanent construction.

◆

Lydford Castle (509848). The massive square structure standing near the church was erected in 1195, and became the infamous Stannary prison.

Okehampton Castle (583942). The present extensive remains, on the west bank of the West Ockment, ruinous since the 16th century, represent buildings which were laid out in the late 13th and the 14th centuries.

Lydford Castle

Okehampton Castle

Part IV
THE PASTORAL AND DOMESTIC SCENE
Dartmoor Architecture

Buildings tend to reflect the geology of the region in which they are located. On and around Dartmoor, as elsewhere, there are dwellings and other structures of alien design and materials, but the traditional building methods of Dartmoor involved the use of local materials - granite and thatch for the most part, with some cob-and-thatch in the area to the north-east bordering on the Culm Measures.

The habitations known as "longhouses" were built to a basic plan which catered for the accommodation of the family at one end and the stock at the other, with a central entrance and passage giving access to both.

A typical granite dwelling of the village and open moor would be long and low, the contour of its roof tending to follow the lie of the land, and the whole blending perfectly with the landscape. The chimney would be massive, the windows modest, with small panes, perhaps with stone mullions and drip-ledges. In the 17th and 18th centuries it was fashionable to have a semi-circular decorated arch over the doorway, which was often set into a massive granite porch, sometimes with a room above.

From the earliest times walls were built of those stones which lay readily available in the immediate vicinity, and in many a derelict building the typical double wall, with rubble filling, can be seen.

There is a feature called broad-and-narrow work, seen in some of the buildings constructed before about 1600, which gave the appearance of massive blocks forming an alternating pattern at the quoins. These were often little more than facing stones, presenting a broad slab-like face, but of little comparative thickness. (This should not be confused with the use of headers and stretchers seen for example at Powder Mills or with long-and-short work, a style used in Anglo-Saxon architecture and therefore not seen in Devon - in this design there were alternating vertical and horizontal blocks at the quoins.)

Some houses in Widecombe parish.
These four dwellings, all within
the space of a mile or so,
illustrate traditional design
in Dartmoor architecture.

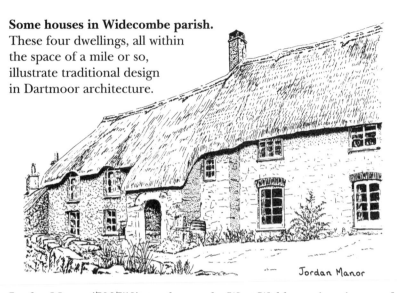

Jordan Manor

Jordan Manor (700750) stands near the West Webburn river, in one of
the numerous hamlets situated within this extensive parish.

Ouldsbroom

Ouldsbroom (or Ollsbrim), at the roadside between Poundsgate and
Dartmeet, with its roof-line very clearly following the slope of the
hillside, is a rare and interesting example of a traditional single-storey
longhouse still in use. It is said to date from about 1600, and stands on
the site of an earlier building. 698734.

Corndon Ford
Farm

Corndon Ford (692745), a working farmstead, lies in the shelter of Corn Down, under Corndon Tor, between Poundsgate and Cator - a case where thatch has given way to slate. The porch bears the date 1718, although the building in general is much older.

Foxworthy (694741), by the same road as Corndon Ford Farm, illustrating again the visual enhancement afforded by the retention of thatch.

Foxworthy

W.C.Thurlow.

Cob and thatch - Bridford

Woodlands Farm (Bridford, 811878), one of the many such farm-houses which lie within the north-east sector of the National Park.

Broad-and-narrow work.
An example of this special
feature of building-design,
seen here at the roadside
in Widecombe village.

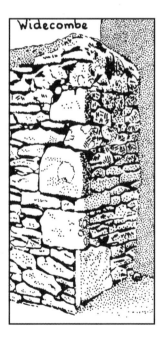

Widecombe

Dunnabridge
Pound Farm

Dunnabridge Pound Farm (Forest, 645746). Corrugated iron, though unsightly, is less expensive than thatch, and serviceable, and was commonly used to cover the latter on dwellings and farm buildings.

◆

A Dartmoor farmyard. The older style of buildings, generally cosier and more substantial than their modern counterparts, tend to be, by comparison, very expensive to maintain.

A dovecote. This little circular building overlooks the A38 road at Pridhamsleigh (749678) between Ashburton and Buckfastleigh. Dovecotes provided both meat and eggs until the late 18th century.

Ash house at West Coombe (North Bovey, 709825). An ash house, of which several examples still exist, provided a convenient repository for ash from domestic fires, and no doubt often a roost for poultry. The accumulated contents were subsequently used as fertiliser.

Hall Farm, Harford

Dovecote – Pridhamsleigh

Ash house – West Coombe

Deserted sites

There are on Dartmoor the remains of numerous modest shelters associated with a variety of pursuits such as tending stock, peat cutting and tinning (although it is not always obvious into which category they fall). At best, all that can now be seen are the low dry-stone walls, with a gap where the entrance would have been, and perhaps the suggestion of a fireplace. Other deserted sites represent more permanent or substantial buildings; the earlier of these have been mentioned.

Many of them, however, were more recent, and the decline of some well-known dwellings, such as the old farmhouse at Nun's Cross, John Bishop's House, and Teignhead farmhouse, has been seen within the last few decades. An account of the erstwhile thriving community associated with Foggintor Quarries, with its various cottages, mission room and school, is given by Kath Brewer in DM Nos 6 and 7 (1987).

The reasons for the abandonment of the sites are of course diverse, but in this connection it is relevant to single out a circumstance whereby numerous farmsteads, some of which had been abandoned for economic reasons, were never re-occupied. This relates to the establishment of the reservoir at Burrator and the substantial number of farms lying within the catchment area.

Lists of deserted sites have been given by Mrs.C.D.Linehan (TDA 97, 1965 - early dwellings and farmsteads) and Brian le Messurier (TDA 111, 1979 - huts and shelters).

———————— ✦ ————————

Newhouse, near Rippon Tor (740755). The inn which stood here, at the roadside between White Gate and Cold East Cross, and just within Ashburton parish, was on an important trade route between Chagford and Ashburton.

Swincombe Cottage, or **Dolly Treble's House** (Forest, 643725), the site of a homestead standing by the old Tavistock-Ashburton track overlooking the Swincombe (right bank) ESE of Swincombe Ford.

Lower Swincombe (Forest, 641726). By the same track, on the opposite bank, lie the ruins of a cottage which takes its alternative name from the expert dry-stone wall builder who lived there.

Newhouse

Swincombe Cottage

John Bishop's House

__ Miscellaneous Stoneware __

Miscellaneous worked stone objects of various shapes and sizes, often abandoned unfinished or broken, are of frequent occurrence, sometimes in the most unlikely places - some of these can present quite a problem as to their original or intended use.

A substantial proportion of the things which attract particular attention are circular stones. It is convenient sometimes to dismiss them as mill stones - probably a fairly safe diagnosis, as mills on Dartmoor have been used over the centuries for a variety of purposes, such as in the production of tin, cider and blasting powder, apart from the processing of grain. It is quite probable, also, that there was a local (and perhaps arbitrary) interest in fashioning millstones for sale elsewhere. There are, however, circular stones which were designed for other applications, including the base-stones of cider - and cheese-presses, and wheelwrights' stones.

Corn mill stones

Discarded corn mill stones, with their characteristic pattern of grooves, can sometimes be seen, lying abandoned, or perhaps used as garden features.

One of the earliest methods of grinding corn was by hand mill or quern. Although querns must have been once in common use, they are now very rare on Dartmoor. Worth's list of several examples was accompanied by a number of detailed drawings; Harry Starkey (1986) selected two others for mention, and Hemery (1983a) noted an unfinished quern at Crazywell Farm. The main body of the device is the part which tends to survive, the upper stone being small and vulnerable. Worth's list includes only one complete quern and three separate upper stones. E.N.Masson Phillips loaned me the photograph for my drawing of a base stone, and drew attention to an upper stone, now in Totnes Museum.

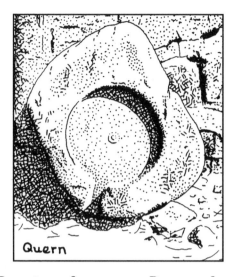

Base stone of a quern at a Dartmoor farm.

Cider mills

A very widespread and pertinent aspect of the pastoral and domestic scene was the manufacture of cider. The remains of cider mills found on the moor usually follow the well-known edge-runner principle, a system which has persisted into modern times in this and other applications - I have first-hand experience of edge-runners in the paint industry, and my grandparents used one to manufacture whiting. The Dartmoor version of this device consists essentially of a large circular stone trough with a socket for a post at the centre. Another stone, set on edge and working on an axle attached to the central post, is made to run round the trough, so crushing the apples within. The juice is extracted in a press, sometimes, but not always of circular plan, and caught in a vat.

It is reasonable to accept that quite a lot of apple-pounding has been accomplished in a variety of other ways, including the use of a domestic mortar (Worth described two in North Bovey Church). An advance on the early methods was the roller mill - by this method the apples were crushed by being passed between two rollers operating side by side.

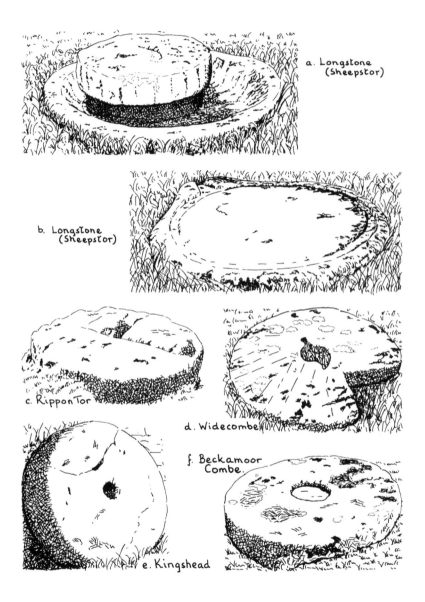

a. Longstone
(Sheepstor)

b. Longstone
(Sheepstor)

c. Rippon Tor

d. Widecombe

e. Kingshead

f. Beckamoor
Combe.

a. **Cider mill at Longstone** (Sheepstor, 556684), one of a number of relics, now plundered, which could be seen near Burrator Reservoir. The edge-runner wheel lay on top of the base stone.

b. **Base of a cider press.** Another of the pieces of cider-making apparatus at Longstone, the circular base of a press, with a peripheral groove and lip for running off the juice.

c. **A stone on Rippon Tor** (Ilsington, 746755), quite likely to have been intended for a millstone, has grooves in a cruciform pattern, which Harry Starkey suggested were cut as part of the process of reducing its thickness. A flaw at the lowest level suggests why the work on it was discontinued.

d. **A millstone** in the garden of a house at Widecombe.

e. **Base-stone of a roundhouse crusher.** A roundhouse is a circular building in which horse- or donkey-power was used to operate a kind of mill for crushing various commodities, or to provide power to drive other apparatus.

f. **A wheelwrights' stone** by the Grimstone and Sortridge Leat in Beckamoor Combe, at the site of the Blacksmiths' Shop (associated with the intensive granite working that went on in that part of the moor). At a time when pack-saddles or "crooks", sleds and other primitive means of transport were being replaced by wheeled carts, and before pneumatic tyres were being applied to rough tracks (main routes were little more) the wheelwright's trade must have been a lucrative one. He used a stone with a large central socket into which the hub fitted whilst the metal tyre was being shrunk onto the rim. There are other examples at the Powder Mills and in Lydford churchyard.

The base of a cider-press at Sourton, seen lying in a private garden next to the green. Enquiry revealed that the pile of miscellaneous stone in which it lay had been brought in, source unknown.

Broken cider mill. This relic, referred to in Crossing's *Guide*, lies a quarter of a mile south-east of Sourton Tors (546895).

A cider vat at the edge of Burrator reservoir, one of the plundered collection of cider-making apparatus at Longstone.

A domestic mortar lying in North Bovey Church, near the south door. (See Worth, pp 389-391). There are some primitive carved designs on its base.

An unfinished quern (?), at Clazywell Farm (Walkhampton, 581700). Hemery was of the opinion that this stone, now lying in the court of the deserted farm site, is an unfinished quern, broken during manufacture. Perhaps, however, it was merely a small mortar.

―――――――― ✦ ――――――――

Troughs

Troughs, both finished and unfinished, are common, though the original purpose of some of them has been argued, e.g. at the "Blacksmiths' Shop" by the Teign (blacksmiths' trough or tinners' mould?), and at "Pigs' House" in Deep Swincombe (tinners' trough or pigs' trough?).

To avoid carrying home excess weight it was obviously better to fashion large items of stoneware on the spot. This accounts for the presence in out of the way places of abandoned pieces broken during dressing. There is, incidentally, at least one case of a perfectly good trough left where it would seem to serve little useful purpose (at Tunhill Rocks).

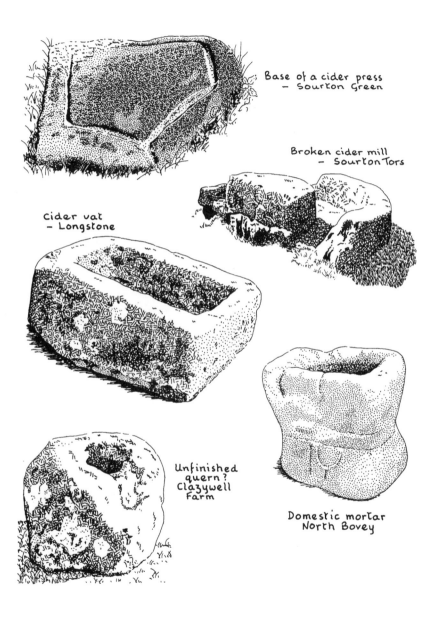

Base of a cider press
 – Sourton Green

Broken cider mill
 – Sourton Tors

Cider vat
 – Longstone

Unfinished
 quern?
Clazywell
 Farm

Domestic mortar
North Bovey

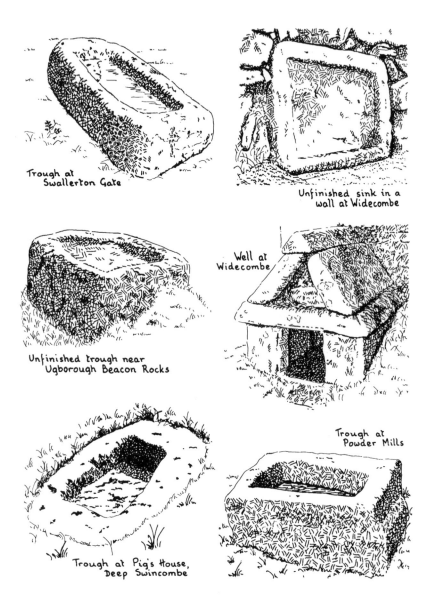

Trough at
Swallerton Gate

Unfinished sink in a
wall at Widecombe

Unfinished trough near
Ugborough Beacon Rocks

Well at
Widecombe

Trough at Pig's House,
Deep Swincombe

Trough at
Powder Mills

Troughs at **Swallerton Gate** (Manaton, 739792), near **Ugborough Beacon Rocks** (667590), **Deep Swincombe** (Forest, 642718), and at the **Powder Mills** (Forest, 627769); and a granite sink built into the roadside wall at the foot of Widecombe Hill (722768).

The old well at Widecombe, by the road to Ponsworthy (717767); I have seen it referred to both as "Saxon" and as "medieval".

———————————— ✦ ————————————

(illustrated overleaf)

The old stocks at Belstone (619936) standing on the village green.

St.Leonard's Well (561676), at the roadside to the east of Sheepstor Church, was used as a domestic water supply until the arrival of mains water.

Upping stocks, consisting of a set of stone steps, designed as an aid to women, in their voluminous skirts, to mount their horses. They are common in Dartmoor villages and hamlets.

The base of a cheese press, lying in Sheepstor churchyard, near the porch (567676). It is incised with a cross, an appropriate symbol here, but in its original application it assisted in the process of running off the whey when pressure was exerted in a wooden cylinder above.

A circular stone among the hut circles and the mass of scattered stone littering the hillside to the east of Merivale Bridge. Until it was recognised as an abandoned cider mill wheel it was thought to be a ruined dolmen. (Walkhampton, 553750.)

St. Leonard's Well, Sheepstor

Stocks at Belstone

Upping stocks -Widecombe

Base of a cheese press- Sheepstor

Cider mill wheel - Merrivale

Walls and Gates

The process of land enclosure has been going on on Dartmoor from prehistoric times, and is still proceeding, unfortunately, at an alarming rate. So long as surface stone was ready to hand in convenient sizes it was natural that such material should be used in the construction of field boundaries and other walls (until it became the fashion, in recent times, to enclose with unsightly, but expedient, fences of posts and wire).

Of particular relevance to Dartmoor's history and topography are the "cornditch" walls which separate the open moorland from the enclosed farmlands. On the side facing the open moor the sheer wall and the accompanying ditch were designed to prevent deer gaining access, whilst their escape from the enclosures was facilitated by a slope up towards the top of the wall on the inside.

In contrast to these and many other such walls (or "hedges") of earth-and-stone construction (such as those bordering the sunken lanes of the in-country) are the open-work dry-stone walls which are such a common feature here. Variations on the theme are manifold; two extremes can be seen facing each other across the highway in the vicinity of the entrance to Prince Hall - comparatively small stone on one side and massive squared blocks on the other. Occasionally substantial boulders ("grounders") have been incorporated into walls of otherwise quite modest members, to provide a firm support.

Where pride in the appearance of a wall was apparently of some account, the side more likely to be seen by passers-by was as neat as could be. The reverse side, however, may not have been aligned with such care (e.g. the wall alongside the track from Two Bridges towards Wistman's Wood). Or is this a variation of the cornditch principle?

The methods by which moorstone was used to provide gateways were various and sometimes ingenious. Examples of slotted and holed gateposts are very numerous. Many have been discarded and built into walls, or relocated and/or fitted with iron pintles to take hinged gates - slotted posts frequently occur as unmatched singles and with the recesses facing in illogical directions. A number of types were classified by R.H.Worth, and, with one amendment, I use his headings here.

"Slip-bar gates" have one feature in common, i.e. the separate wooden rails were each first inserted into simple slots in one of the posts. The principal variation comes in the manner in which the other ends of the rails were fitted to the second post:

Slot-and-L gates. There is a series of inverted L-shaped slots into each of which a rail was pushed and dropped.

Slot-and taper gates. The rails were lowered from above into slots of increasing depth. Worth called these posts "slot-and-arc", referring to a curved back to the slots, but the latter are uncommon variants - straight-backed tapers are more usual, and common.

Locked-bar gates. The rails were lodged in corner recesses, and held in place by an upright bar which was secured by means of a fastener such as a slot, eye and wedge.

Double-slot gates. The first post had slots of double depth, into which the rails were pushed. The latter were then reversed into slots of standard depth in the second post.

———————————— ✦ ————————————

"Holed-stone" gatehangers

There was a system by means of which a wooden gate of essentially conventional design was pivoted using a socketed stone, or "holed-stone", gatehanger. A long and substantial stone was laid along the top of a wall with its end, containing a downward-facing socket, overhanging the gateway. The especially-long upper end of the stanchion of the gate was located in the socket, and an iron peg, which was fitted to the bottom of the stanchion, pivoted in a hole in a stone at ground level. An upper stone remains in position at the side of the by-road from Uppacott (Poundsgate) to Locks Gate Cross, a few yards from the highway, but most such stones have been discarded or put to other uses. An example now standing by the Mariners' Way near Yardworthy also contains slots associated with a slip-bar gate. There is a rebuilt system at Peck Farm, Lustleigh (762826) (see Dave Brewer, DM No 20), but there is perhaps now only one surviving example of a "holed-stone" gate as originally installed (near Cox Tor), and here the stanchion completely pierces the hanger.

The holed-stone principle has also been used to hang doors and windows.

(illustrated overleaf)

A cattle grid and gate, the present-day arrangement which allows for the unrestricted passage of motorised traffic whilst controlling the movement of animals on the hoof. (Chagford, 680849.)

A stile near Rundlestone Corner (Forest, 575749) constructed of stones of regular shape.

A gatepost near Princetown (Forest, 593739). The holes may have been made with the intention of splitting the post, but their elliptical shape is not normally associated with this process.

Discarded gateposts. The granite posts once in use at Hemsworthy Gate lay for a period at the roadside nearby. (Approximately on the Widecombe/Ilsington boundary.)

Detail of a wall alongside the road from Tawton Gate to Fernworthy, containing large moorstones trigged up in typical style with smaller pieces. (Chagford, 6784.)

The wall of Muddilakes Newtake, alongside the Ashburton-Two Bridges road, was made (by John Bishop of Swincombe, it is said), using large regular blocks - an advance on the age-old system to be seen across the road. (Forest, 6174.)

The Swincombe valley above Hexworthy, seen from the northern slope of Ter Hill (Forest, 6372.)

A cornditch wall (Lydford, 531857) near High Down Ford, a case where more than casual attention was given to the selection and arrangement of the stones.

A granite post at Teignhead Farm - obviously something more than simple wall construction. There are some impressive slotted gateposts at this site. (Forest, 634842.)

A sheep creep, provided in order to allow sheep to negotiate a wall without affording the same facility to larger beasts, within enclosures near Bel Tor (Widecombe, 695730.)

A cornditch wall near the Bovey (Chagford, 683834), opposite Hurston Castle, where there is a common form of construction, with basic stability afforded by the use of a framework of "grounders".

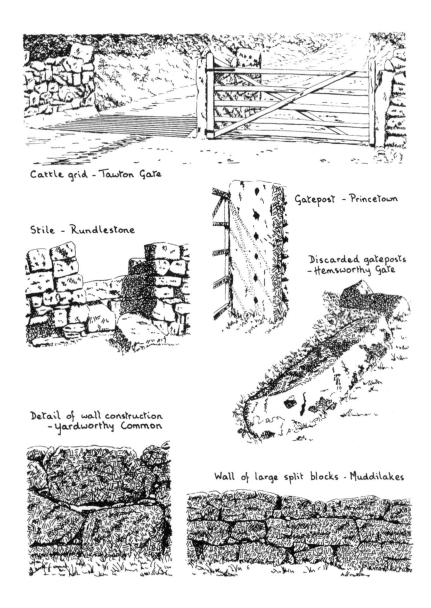

Cattle grid - Tawton Gate

Gatepost - Princetown

Stile - Rundlestone

Discarded gateposts - Hemsworthy Gate

Detail of wall construction - Yardworthy Common

Wall of large split blocks - Muddilakes

Gateway above the Swincombe

Cornditch wall - High Down

A massive post - Teignhead Farm

Sheep creep - Bel Tor

Stone gatehanger
used in wall building

Stone
gatehanger

Hunting
gate

"Slot-and-L"
gateposts

Stone stile

A
step-
stile

Typical dry-stone wall

"Holed-stone" gatehangers. Top left is a socketed stone taken from its original use and incorporated into a wall (at the crossroads between Jordan and Dockwell - Widecombe, 701753). Top right, the system still in use, at Coxtor Farm, Peter Tavy (520760).

A hunting gate, which allows a rider to pass without dismounting, is of sufficient size for other purposes so long as access is not required for wheeled traffic. (Water Rushes, Ashburton. 745738.)

A stile, near Hammerslake, Lustleigh, with an unworked and markedly curved slab used as a bar. (774816.)

Slot-and-L gateposts. The slots were cut to accept separate bars or "latches" - their number and arrangement could be altered to suit immediate requirements depending upon the measure of security demanded. These posts (at Manaton, 750811) are typical in that they were later modified to take a hinged gate.

A step-stile in the wall of the prison enclosures near Rundlestone Corner (Forest, 579749).

A typical dry-stone wall (near White Gate, 7476), one stone deep and showing the open-work effect imparted by this style of construction.

Top row

Left: A post with tapered slots, at a gateway near the edge of the down above **Dockwell** (Widecombe, 703759). The matching post is at the next gate a few yards away.

Centre: A pair of "slot-and-taper" posts still in a paired situation, in the stroll which leads to the site of **Emsworthy Farm** (Ilsington, 746765). There are several posts of this type related to the enclosures of the farm.

Right: A rough pillar, with slots in its receding face, at the roadside 250 yards west of **Rowden** (Widecombe, 697765).

Middle row

Left: A gatepost at the roadside 200 yards west of **Lewthorn Cross** (Ilsington, 777761); it barely qualifies as a representative of Worth's elusive "slot-and-arc" type.

Centre and right: Posts of the "locked-bar" type, 150 yards west of **Rowden** (698764) and at the roadside on **Widecombe Hill** (723768).

Bottom row

Left: A "double-slot" gatepost, one of a pair near **Hoo Meavy Bridge;** this post has slots twice the usual depth. 526656.

Centre: A disused post at **Hisley Bridge** (Lustleigh, 780800), with a set of "locked-bar" recesses and a set of normal sockets.

Right: A post which contains the socket of a "holed-stone" gatehanger and also a set of slots, overlooking the South Teign 300 yards north of **Yardworthy** (Chagford, 679854).

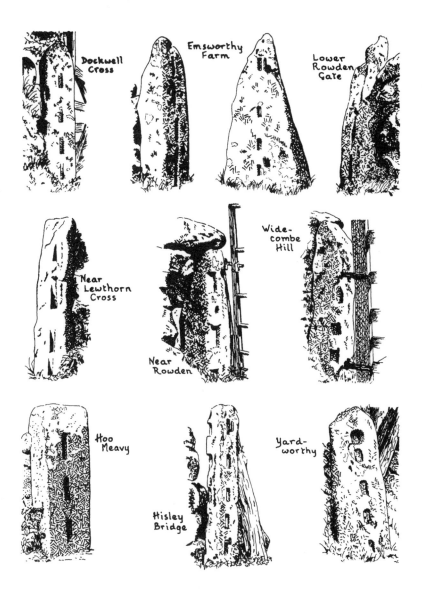

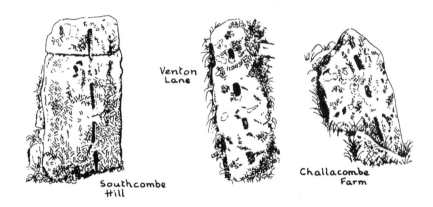

Venton Lane

Southcombe Hill

Challacombe Farm

Gateposts: Variation in length of slots.

Left: Long slots at the side of the road leading up from Widecombe to **Dunstone Down** (711764).

Centre: Short slots at a gateway between the **Rugglestone Inn** and Venton (721763).

Right: Slots of different lengths in one post; one of a pair straddling a fence at the roadside a short distance below **Blue Gate** (676761).

Stiles

"Wood-and-stone" stiles are similar in concept to the double-slot slip-bar gates described above, but the wooden rails are not movable, so the design required the rails and second post to be put in place in one operation. A pair of such posts stands where a footpath from Manaton Church emerges on to the road to the west (746812), the "stop-gap" nature of the existing woodwork illustrating the inflexibility of this design. Another pair stands at the entrance to the woods on the east side of New Bridge (Holne, 711708).

Stiles made entirely of stone are to be found in a virtually "sliding scale" of designs, of which the most primitive may be almost indistinguishable from a collapsed piece of walling. Among the carefully erected examples there is a pattern consisting essentially of four rough slabs of which two, the uprights, are each provided with a vertical and a horizontal groove to accommodate the sill and the step. A "de luxe" edition of this design has carefully squared components with accurate mortises, tenons and rebates.

The "step-stile" is not uncommon; this design utilises stones fitted so as to project from the wall in a "staircase" pattern.

Modern stiles tend to be made entirely of wood, because of the ease of fabrication and the durability afforded by the use of efficiently treated timber. Apart from the varieties of more universal "standard" design, the "ladder-stile" (like a stepladder straddling a wall or fence) has been installed in places, to negotiate a barrier without structural interference.

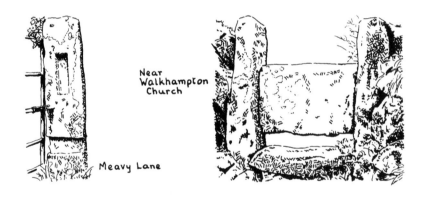

Near Walkhampton Church

Meavy Lane

Left: A squared pillar which formed part of a stone stile, re-used as a gatepost, in **Meavy Lane** (535675). A squared post opposite the entrance to Walreddon (Whitchurch, 478813) has an additional vertical slot beneath the horizontal groove.

Right: One of the stiles in the vicinity of **Walkhampton Church** (this one is on the path which goes towards Holwell Farm). The four basic components are rough slabs, the only refinements being the jointing construction.

___ Drift and Manor Pounds ___

Not to be confused with the enclosures used by prehistoric peoples, the drift and manor pounds were established in connection with the management of stock in and around the Forest. Erme Pound (Harford, 638656), which covers about an acre and a quarter above the stream from which it takes its name, appears originally to have been a prehistoric enclosure- it is irregular in shape and there are hut circles within it. It was put into use in medieval times as one of the Duchy "drift" pounds, in which illegally depastured cattle and ponies were impounded.

There are other pounds of great antiquity (though not necessarily prehistoric) of which Dunnabridge Pound (Forest, 646746), at the roadside between Dartmeet and Two Bridges, and covering an area of about 2 ½ acres, is the best example, being still functional and impressive.

Halstock pound (Okehampton, 603930), second in importance to Dunnabridge, is a small rectangular enclosure; it is not clear whether its original use was a manor or drift pound.

Creber Pound (Gidleigh, 663881) is merely a space between farm enclosures, and whilst gated at the moorland end is no longer so at the other end and cannot be recognised as a pound.

Besides the Duchy pounds there are numerous small manor pounds such as those at Gidleigh and Poundsgate.

Gidleigh Pound (672884) is an ancient manor pound which borders the road to the north of the village church.

Hut at Erme Pound. To the outside of the pound are the remains of two little buildings which may have served as shelters at the time of the drifts. The smaller one, near the gateway, is furnished with a low stone bench.

Dunnabridge Pound contains a shelter known as the Judge's Chair, the origin of which has caused a lot of speculation in the past. Crossing discusses the theory that it may have been brought from the site of the tinners' parliament at Crockern Tor (there was probable confusion with a slab of stone at Dunnabridge Farm), and that it had been the seat of an Arch-druid. (The Victorian idea of fervent druidical activity on Dartmoor has long been considered rather far-fetched). He came to the conclusion that it was, in fact a dolmen; this idea, though more tenable, is also open to question.

Gidleigh Pound

Hut with benches - Erme Pound

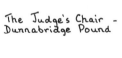

The Judge's Chair - Dunnabridge Pound

——— Places of Worship ———

On approaching the National Park boundary in the vicinity of Dart Bridge, two churches with singular features come into view. The parish church of The Holy Trinity, Buckfastleigh, standing high above the town, is the only Dartmoor church with a spire (though there is a similar feature on St. Lawrence's Tower at Ashburton). Buckfast Abbey, nearby, was painstakingly rebuilt by the Benedictine monks, between 1880 and 1938, on the site of a much earlier building. It has close connections with the moor, as had the abbeys at Tavistock and Buckland, and the priory at Plympton. On the western side, the Church of St. Michael, Brentor, is unique by reason of its diminutive size and its position, being conspicuously sited on a conical hill (a resistant ridge composed of volcanic breccia and pillow lava - the latter exuded under a former sea).

Between these extremes of situation and character lie the typical moorland parish churches. Here and there in the landscape of the in-country the tower of a moorstone church comes into view, quite often embellished with four corner pinnacles, a special feature of many Dartmoor churches, and from high viewpoints churches such as that at Buckland in the Moor can be seen nestling in their wooded surroundings far below.

Dartmoor was not overlooked by the Wesleyan movement in the West Country in the mid-eighteenth century, and signs of its influence within the moor are seen in the little Methodist chapels at Poundsgate and Peatcot. There are other ways in which Dartmoor history has been coloured by the ups and downs of religious life - for example, the clergy were not immune from the depredations of the Black Death, and Puritanism took its toll of the interior furnishings of churches here as elsewhere.

We may be reminded of the former existence of religious buildings by the stones marking the outlines of the walls as at the Mission Room (Walkhampton, 567750) between Rundlestone Corner and Merivale, or by a name on a map as at St. Michael's Chapel, Halstock. Tavistock Abbey and Plympton Priory are now represented by fragmentary ruins, and Buckland Abbey (Buckland Monachorum, 487668), restored and altered over the years, became a dwelling house, occupied for a time by Sir Francis Drake, and is now a museum.

There are over forty churches within the National Park, and my illustrations include about a third of them, concentrating on their exteriors, particularly their towers, the features by which they can be recognised in the landscape.

The **Chapel of St. Mary,** by the old Exeter-Okehampton road in the parish of South Tawton (650936), was built perhaps as a guild chapel for the weavers, tuckers and fullers of South Zeal. The present building dates from the late 15th century. There were later renovations, and in its time the chapel has served as a school and the schoolmaster's house, eventually becoming a chapel-of-ease to South Tawton in 1877.

South Zeal

(illustrated overleaf)
Peatcot Wesley Chapel (Forest, 605714), built by the Worth family in 1912 in a remote situation north-west of Whiteworks, is approached by way of Castle Road from Princetown.

St. Michael de Rupe, Brentor (471804), a tiny Norman church, is over 1000 feet above sea level and is a prominent landmark over much of West Devon.

Holy Trinity, Buckfastleigh (742666). Dating from the 13th and 15th centuries, the church was drastically restored in 1845. The ruins of a 13th century chantry chapel stand to the east in the churchyard. Opposite the porch there is a tomb contained within an iron-barred cell; such were the precautions thought necessary, it seems, to curb the activities of Richard Cabell, the model of Conan Doyle's wicked squire in "The Hound of the Baskervilles". The church was gutted by fire 21st July 1992.

St. Raphael's, Huccaby (Forest, 663730), a modest building at the roadside opposite Huccaby Farm, Hexworthy, was erected in 1869 to serve as a mission chapel and schoolroom.

Peatcot Wesley Chapel

St. Michael's, Brentor

Buckfastleigh

St. Raphael's, Huccaby

(illustrated overleaf)
Sheepstor Church (dedication unknown, possibly St. Leonard). 560676. The church lies to the south of Burrator Reservoir and is dominated by the great hill from which the village takes its name. There is an interesting old sun-dial plate, carved in stone, over the south porch, and nearby is a circular stone with an incised cross (see Miscellaneous stoneware). In the churchyard are the tombs of Sir James Brooke and his nephew, White Rajahs of Sarawak.

St. Mary the Virgin, Holne. 706695. The plain rough-cast tower of the medieval church is no advertisement for the attraction of the main building and the treasures within. These include a beautifully carved screen and a very fine pulpit. There is a memorial window to Charles Kingsley, who was born in the Vicarage.

Holy Trinity, Gidleigh (671884) is approachable by way of the network of minor roads which reticulate the north-east sector of the National Park, and lies within a mile of the open moor. At the road junction beyond the pound there is a gatepost in the shape of a pinnacle - a probable link with the absence of pinnacles on the tower.

Walkhampton Church (dedication unknown). 536701. From the high ground to the north-east of Yelverton the eye is attracted by the very prominent tower rising amid the farmlands of the border country. Nearby is the 16th century manor house.

St. Pancras, Widecombe in the Moor (718768), "the cathedral of the moor", was said to have been built from the wealth of the tinners (there is a "tinners' rabbits" roof-boss - see page 207). The tower, though disproportionately high, fits perfectly into the landscape of the Widecombe valley. There is a board inside relating the story of the great thunderstorm of 1638.

Sheepstor

Holne

Gidleigh

Walkhampton

Widecombe

W. G. Thurlow.

(illustrated overleaf)

St. Petrock's, Lydford (509847), standing near the castle keep, is mainly of the 15th century, and has a fine modern screen and bench-ends. In the churchyard a watchmaker's epitaph is worth noticing, and there is a wheelwrights' stone. At the gate there is an interesting old milestone.

St. John the Baptist, Leusdon. 709732. The church, in the parish of Widecombe, was built in 1863. The tower comes into view as one gains the top of Newbridge Hill, and its situation, high above Lizwell Meet in the Webburn valley, is superb.

St. Mary's, Sampford Spiney. 534725. The 14th century church is situated by the green in this small hamlet (there is no village). The arms of Plympton priory are on the tower.

St. Peter's, Buckland in the Moor. 720731. The original building and its later development cover a period between the late 12th and the late 16th centuries. The beginning and end of this period are marked, respectively, by the font and the very notable carved and painted rood-screen. The design of the memorial tower clock-face is ingenious, with the letters of "My dear mother" taking the place of numerals.

St. Michael's, Chagford. 701875. The tower pinnacles (similar to the gatepost mentioned in connection with Gidleigh church) were taken down in the middle of this century and were not replaced. The church has some interesting interior features, including a "tinners' rabbits" roof-boss.

St. Mary the Virgin, Throwleigh. 668907. A mile and a half to the north of Gidleigh, the church is similarly close to the open moor. The priest's doorway is worthy of note, as are the screen and pulpit.

Holy Trinity, Drewsteignton (736908), standing high above the Teign gorge near the northern boundary of the National Park, dates from the 15th and 16th centuries, but its most notable furnishings, the pews with their carved bench-ends, are very recent, emphasising the local influence of the Drewe family of Castle Drogo.

St. Michael and All Angels, Princetown. Princetown is in the Forest, which was until the boundary changes of 1987 an extensive attachment to the otherwise modest parish of Lydford. Lydford had its own parish church centuries before Princetown came into existence. The Princetown church was built and furnished by prisoners of war during the early years of the 19th century, the building by the Americans and the furnishings by the French.

Lydford

Leusdon

Sampford Spiney

Buckland in the Moor

Chagford

Throwleigh

Drewsteignton

Princetown

Inns

In and around Dartmoor, as elsewhere, the name of a village can be almost synonymous with that of its inn - I mentioned Christow to a friend, his response was "Oh, the Artichoke!". However, the inns of Dartmoor have become far fewer than they were in the days of thirsty travel and untreated water. One of the best-known of those that are gone was New House between Hemsworthy Gate and Cold East Cross; and though some newer ones have appeared, we sometimes learn of their predecessors, such as the Greyhound at Postbridge and the Saracen's Head at Two Bridges.

Many of the inns have a special interest of one kind or another. The Warren House Inn, for example (named after Headland Warren), has its fair share of stories, in this land of folk-lore and legend, whilst there are others (though less isolated perhaps) which are equally well-known, probably because of their aesthetic appeal or the convenience of their situation. Among these are the Tavistock Inn at Poundsgate and the Dartmoor Inn at Merrivale. The Forest Inn at Hexworthy is another, now a substantial and conspicuous structure, a far cry from the modest thatched building it replaced (illustrated in Crossing's *Dartmoor Worker*).

If we look for architectural appeal, the Oxenham Arms at South Zeal and the Three Crowns at Chagford are unsurpassed.

(illustrated overleaf)
Warren House Inn (Forest, 674809), said to be the third highest inn in England, stands by the Moretonhampstead to Two Bridges road near King's Oven and just within the Forest. The present building replaced an inn known as New House which stood on the opposite side of the road and in which a visitor discovered a corpse, salted-in and awaiting the disappearance of the snow which had prevented the long journey for burial.

The Rugglestone Inn (720765), 400 yards south-east of Widecombe Church, and tucked away at a bend in the road to Venton, is noted for its small size. It takes its name from a nearby logan stone.

Two Bridges Hotel (Forest, 608749) stands near the confluence of the Cowsic and the West Dart, where the trans-moor highways intersect, at the site of an earlier inn.

Warren House Inn

The Rugglestone Inn

Two Bridges Hotel

Part V
WATER, THE GREAT RESOURCE

Drawing water from a well, whilst a fairly universal basic method of water extraction, has its own particular Dartmoor connotation, in that here a well is normally a spring. There are a number of such named wells out on the open moor. William's Well, for example, gives rise to a tiny feeder of Blackslade Water near the Tunhill Track. Fitz's Well, by the Blackabrook, being situated in a fairly remote area, is favoured in being protected by a low shelter (it is also contained within a low enclosure wall). Such shelters are a normal feature of wells in home locations; many of these sources, such as St. Leonard's Well at Sheepstor and the well by the road at Widecombe, are now out of use.

Short of the immediate proximity of a "well" or stream it has rarely been a very great problem to get water to isolated farms and dwellings; they would in any case have been established within a reasonable distance of running water, and introducing a supply into the premises was merely a matter of constructing a pot-water leat from the stream or from another leat.

Leats were used for centuries to provide water to operate the early tinning and later mining machinery, and for other industrial purposes (eventually to include some small hydro-electric schemes).

There are some very long leats which operated in connection with mine workings, such as the Vitifer Mine and Wheal Emma, but the most ambitious were those which conveyed water to Plymouth and Devonport.

The Plymouth Leat was constructed towards the end of the 16th century, under the guidance of Sir Francis Drake, to take water from the Meavy to Plymouth, a distance of 18 ½ miles. Its headweir is now submerged under Burrator Reservoir.

When Plymouth Dock, later to become known as Devonport, was expanded two centuries later an additional supply was needed (such facilities weren't shared in those days), and another leat was constructed (completed in about 1801), this time over a distance of 27 miles.

The Devonport Leat is probably the best-known of the Dartmoor man-made water-courses. Its history is one of development, modification and partial obsolescence. As functional at present, it takes water from the West Dart, Cowsic, Blackabrook, and the Hart Tor Brook/ Meavy confluence, and disappears ultimately alongside the disused track of the GWR Yelverton-Princetown Branch, above the Yelverton Reservoir and the Burrator Reservoir dam. Some of the flow descends by an attractive waterfall at the roadside here (what a pity the ugly pipe is not camouflaged!). (There is also a cascade down the side of Raddick Hill, visible from the Yelverton-Princetown road.)

One of the modifications of the Devonport Leat involved the shortening of the West Dart-Cowsic section by about a mile. The flow was diverted by pipeline over a stone aqueduct, creating one of the most attractive views on the moor; it rejoins the original leat by means of a fountain (north of the Tavistock road west of Two Bridges).

The Blackabrook crossing is within the prison enclosures and therefore not accessible to the general public. (John Robins was able to obtain special permission and in his book *Rambling On* records the results of his investigations in this area.)

The course of the now obsolete Plymouth (or Drake's) Leat and the disused section of the Devonport Leat can be traced here and there beyond the Burrator area - for example, the dry channel of the Plymouth Leat is easily seen where the road from Burrator meets that from Dousland to Meavy village.

✦

The Devonport Leat. The drawing illustrates in diagrammatic form the currently functional part of the leat. Whilst the intakes are in fact in almost a straight line, running approximately NE-SW, a distance of over 6 miles, the leat travels much further than this as it contours the hillsides.

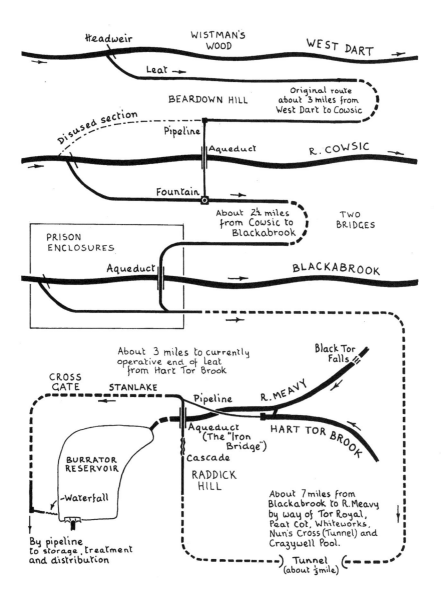

Aqueduct and sluice gate. Under Raddick Hill the Devonport Leat crosses the Meavy by way of the "Iron Bridge" (Walkhampton, 573713) where a further supply is taken in to augment its volume.

A tunnel by means of which the Devonport Leat negotiates the hill between Nun's Cross Farm and Drivage Bottom. (Walkhampton/ Forest, 6069.)

A bullseye. The volume of supply into a subsidiary leat can be maintained at an optimum level by the use of a sluice or a "bullseye" - a hole in a stone set into the side of the main channel. The example shown here no longer serves its original purpose. (Sheepstor churchyard.)

Stone near Lud Gate (Buckfastleigh, 682673). Near the Huntingdon Mine track a short distance on to the moor there is a stone penetrated by a fairly large hole, which may have been associated with controlling water-flow.

◆

(illustrated overleaf)
Fice's (or **Fitz's**) **Well** (Forest, 577758) (not to be confused with Fitz's Well, Okehampton) is below the track of the Princetown peat tramway (which can be followed northwards from the highway near Rundlestone Corner). The structure is said to have been erected by John Fitz as a token of gratitude after he and his lady, lost on the moor, rediscoverd their path following a drink from the spring. The roof slab is inscribed "IF 1568".

A capped borehole (Walkhampton, 576716), one of several in the valley of Hartor Brook, associated with investigations into finding a site for a reservoir for Plymouth; Burrator was ultimately chosen.

A bullseye near the stone cross north of Feather Tor, where a branch supply is abstracted from the Grimstone and Sortridge Leat (Whitchurch, 534743).

Aqueduct
(the Iron
Bridge)
(R. Meavy).

A sluice gate

A bullseye (Sheepstor).

Tunnel - near Nun's Cross

Holed stone
- near
Lud Gate
(Buckfast-
leigh)

Fice's Well

Capped borehole
- Hartor Brook

Bullseye -
Windy Post

An advance in the means of water extraction over the simple weir and leat was the installation of more substantial intakes. A typical example may be approached by way of a service road or track along a valley side, and will have a weir of sufficient size to create a small reservoir. There will probably be, unfortunately, an unsightly display of concrete walls and iron grills, and the most conspicuous feature is likely to be a little square hut, standing stark and incongruous in a beautiful landscape.

Some of these intakes have been either superseded by, or used as an adjunct to the ultimate means of water collection, the major reservoirs, which are at Burrator, Venford, Dean Moor, a group of three in the Hennock/Christow area, Fernworthy and Meldon. Few can deny the beauty of some of these man-made lakes. There are some redeeming features at Burrator, for example - the site is on the edge of enclosed farmland, thus there is a little native tree cover in the locality between the incongruous conifer plantations, and the dam was constructed during a period when a mellowing granite facing was considered to be a reasonable detail of construction. Little, however, can ever soften the visual injury inflicted by the gross and undisguised concrete dams (and their associated treatment works) related to today's economic and constructional standards, particularly when the reservoirs are situated on the open moor. The occasional screens of conifers may be considered attractive, and the rhododendrons are certainly so, but both are out of character in an open moor context, and the latter could become a tiresome pest.

A project in the 1950s to extract water from Taw Marsh was complicated by the presence in the water of radon gas (in recent years a factor of increasing concern in the granite country of the south-west). However, $2\frac{1}{2}$ million gallons a day are extracted from shallow wells there and suitably treated. The latest reservoir, at Meldon, constructed amid considerable controversy, flooded a valley of outstanding beauty; and plans for yet another reservoir - on the Swincombe at Fox Tor Mire, a desolate area in the southern moor - were shelved only after a long and bitter struggle between opposing factions.

(illustrated overleaf)
The Avon Dam (South Brent/Dean Prior, 679651) is accessible (to pedestrians) by way of the waterworks road from Shipley Bridge (1 $\frac{1}{2}$. miles). Was there an opportunity here of creating a more agreeable scene, to compensate in some measure for the loss of a beautiful valley?

Headweir of the Wheal Friendship Leat. The leat is taken in from the Tavy in the Cleave (549830), and comes down over Nattor Down, near Lanehead (Peter Tavy).

Water Board Stones indicate the boundaries of the catchment areas around the reservoirs. The example shown, at the roadside on Holne Moor (690706), is one of those above Venford Reservoir; these particular pillars mark the limits of the land bought by Paignton UDC (about 1900) from Richard Dawson, then Lord of the Manor.

A waterworks hut (South Brent, 680640) above Shipley Bridge. A stark intrusion into the landscape, and a case where the viability of landscaping could be debated.

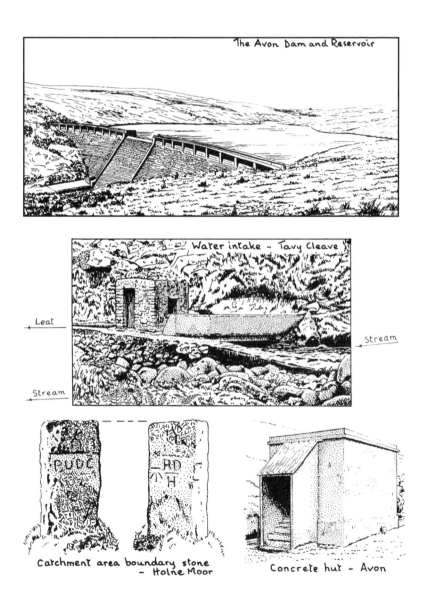

The Avon Dam and Reservoir

Water intake - Tavy Cleave

Leat

Stream

Stream

Catchment area boundary stone
- Holne Moor

Concrete hut - Avon

Some details of the major reservoirs

Avon Dam (Dean Prior/South Brent, 6765). R.Avon (and Brockhill Water). Completed 1957. Area 50 acres. Capacity 305m glns.

Burrator (Meavy/Sheepstor/Walkhampton, 5568). R.Meavy (and Narrator Brook, Venney Lake and Devonport Leat). 1898; expanded 1928. 150 acres. 1026m glns.

Fernworthy (Chagford/Forest, 6684). South Teign (and Assacombe Brook, Lowton Brook, Shute Lake and Longstone Brook). 1942. 76 acres. 380m glns. Pipeline to Trenchford.

Meldon (Okehampton Hamlets, 5691). West Okement (and Fishcombe Water). 1972 . 54 acres. 680m glns.

Venford (Holne, 6870). Venford Brook (and pipeline from Swincombe, and Holne Moor Leat from O Brook). 1907. 33 acres. 198m glns.

The Hennock reservoirs . Kennick Brook, Trenchford Stream (and pipeline from Fernworthy to Trenchford):

> *Tottiford* (Christow/Hennock, 8183). 1861; embankments raised 1866, 1867. 31 acres. 103m glns.
>
> *Kennick* (Bridford/Christow, 8084). 1884. 52 acres. 195m glns.
>
> *Trenchford* (Hennock/Bovey Tracey, 8082). 1907. 30 acres. 171m glns.

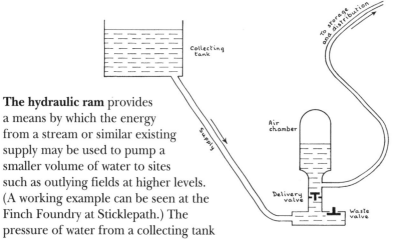

The hydraulic ram provides a means by which the energy from a stream or similar existing supply may be used to pump a smaller volume of water to sites such as outlying fields at higher levels. (A working example can be seen at the Finch Foundry at Sticklepath.) The pressure of water from a collecting tank forces the waste valve shut and opens the delivery valve. The lowering of pressure then opens the waste valve and shuts the delivery valve. The air in the air chamber acts like a compression spring and forces water up the delivery pipe. The alternating reversal of opposing forces produces a rhythmic pumping action.

Part VI
HIGHWAYS AND BY-WAYS
Tracks

Over much of Dartmoor the nature of the terrain has always limited the use of wheeled traffic, and there was a time when the heavier loads were carried by packhorse, sledge or perhaps truck-a-muck. In some places the continuous wear of a restricted path produced a drainage channel, thus inducing accelerated erosion. (This process continues, and is a relevant factor in assessing the impact of an ever-increasing walking and riding public.) In those places where the going was easier it was not necessary to stick to a narrow way. Thus, while some routes are well-marked here and there by sunken tracks, there are some which are difficult to follow. Crossing described a total of eighty-one "packhorse and other old paths", and these he regarded as only the principal ones. Most of them have no special name, apart perhaps from that of their destination. The named tracks include the King Way, the Dartmoor Path, Sandy Way, Church Way, Mariners' Way, Drift Lane and Cut Lane.

One of the most important tracks is the Lich Path; this route was used by people residing in the eastern part of the Forest, in their travels to and from their parish church at Lydford. (Its name is related to its use for carrying the dead for burial - as in "lychgate".)

The Jobbers' Path was apparently used by wool-jobbers - people who carried wool by packhorse train; and the two Black Lanes and Blackwood Path alluded to their use for the transport of peat.

Whether or not the name "Abbots' Way" is historically valid, the concept of a route linking the abbey at Buckfast with the religious houses of Tavistock and Buckland on the other side of the moor is a reasonable one, and it is not unlikely that the monks made use of earlier tracks. A spongy but relatively direct route across the moor might have been preferable to the rocky and often muddy gullies which served as tracks round the perimeter. In this connection, there is a series of old stone crosses, of which about a dozen are on open moorland between Holne and Walkhampton; and there seems to have been a series between Plympton and Tavistock, and another between

Moretonhampstead and Postbridge.

In *Walking Dartmoor's Ancient Tracks* Eric Hemery (1986) described twenty-eight routes in considerable detail, with accompanying maps.

Walking "into the interior" (colloquially "out over") can be facilitated in some areas by the use of more modern tracks, such as the disused Red Lake Railway in the south, and the military tracks branching out from Okehampton Moor Gate in the north.

Roads

The history of the development of roads as we know them, on and around Dartmoor, began in the second half of the eighteenth century. Responsibility for their maintenance once fell to the various parishes through which they ran, but from about 1750 turnpike trusts were set up, associated with numerous Acts of Parliament, by means of which a less piecemeal system was operated, improvement being assisted by the use of revenue from toll-gates. The octagonal appearance of a number of dwellings still standing at roadsides around the moor betrays their earlier use as toll-houses.

There are some roadside stones relating to the limits adopted by the trusts. The best-known of these, by the A386 road north of Lower Beardon (518843), is inscribed "Take off" - it was up to this point that an additional horse was allowed without extra charge to assist in pulling a load uphill. Dave Brewer, (in his *Guide* and in DAS Newsletter No 36) has recorded further stones of this type, and others more clearly related to the trusts.

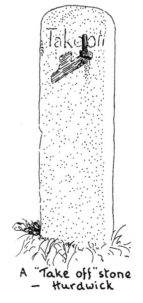

A "Take off" stone
— Hurdwick

The **"Take off stone"** at Hurdwick (Mary Tavy) now stands close to the house (having been recovered from its use as a gatepost). 472758.

The perimeter roads were turnpiked first, attention being given later to routes across the moor. During this period some re-routing of old tracks took place; and in this connection it is interesting to reflect that, with the advent of modern transport, at least one straight path was "bent" to ease a gradient - the highway which ascends Dartmeet Hill now describes a curve, whilst the old track which preceded it goes straight up, by the Coffin Stone. New methods of surfacing were introduced, and when the coming of the railways put an end to the turnpike system the care of the roads became the responsibility of the county.

The countless "Devon lanes" of the border country are for the most part single-track and frequently sunken (to which can often be added "steep and serpentine") and the occasional protruding rock is a potential hazard. (In a few places the main highways are little better).

———————— ✦ ————————

The **Moretonhampstead-Yelverton highway,** a good motor road (with a few moderate gradients), offers extensive views of open moorland. From this viewpoint, south-west of Princetown, we see Sharp Tor (one of several Sharps), Leedon Tor and Ingra Tor.

The size of vehicles is restricted on the other trans-moor highway between Ashburton and Dartmeet because of conditions which include the narrow bendy stretch through Poundsgate, and narrow bridges (New Bridge, and Holne Bridge with its associated right-angle bends), but this road is not normally difficult for the average private car.

A Devon lane. The ease (or otherwise) of vehicular access to Dartmoor locations is infinitely variable. Burrator, the most picturesque of Dartmoor reservoirs, is a locality which can be approached from a number of directions. However, on some of these routes a driver can have problems when meeting other traffic. The drawing illustrates the nature of the road which goes by way of Lowery Cross and Cross Gate - not designed for modern traffic - where protruding fence posts make the way seem even narrower. (There is an unrestricted approach to Burrator from the Dousland end - second left beyond the skyline in the top picture.)

Unfenced road
— Walkhampton Common

Near Burrator Reservoir
— a typical narrow lane

___ Railways and Tramways ___

Mainline rail services between Paddington and Penzance continue to run on the old GWR system along the moor's southern edge, penetrating the National Park only in the vicinity of South Brent. The only other relevant surviving stretch of permanent way serves to take stone from Meldon Quarry towards Exeter via Okehampton and Crediton; this is the old Southern Railway line that linked Plymouth with London (Waterloo) via Tavistock and Lydford. There are some quite lengthy disused sections of track that run within the National Park on the western side.

Of the old railways which once served the moor, the Princetown line disappeared amid an atmosphere of regret. The Plymouth and Dartmoor railway (of 4½ ft gauge), which began as a mineral tramroad to transport stone from Foggintor Quarry, was superseded by the Princetown Branch of the Great Western Railway, using the same line but with amended curves to render it suitable for steam traction. The railway, which would eventually have been an increasingly important, and no doubt remunerative attraction, was closed because it was uneconomic; the last train ran in October 1956.

The Ashburton Branch of the old GWR from Totnes (the Dart Valley line) is now represented by that section which goes from Totnes to Buckfastleigh, and run privately as a visitor attraction. The terminal stretch, where the line approximated to the National Park boundary between Buckfastleigh and Ashburton, is gone - the A38 road now runs over its course. Another branch line ran from Newton Abbot to Moretonhampstead via Bovey Tracey and Lustleigh, along the beautiful Wray valley. (At Bovey Tracey it has been used for the town by-pass.)

A number of industrial undertakings had their own railways and tramways. Railways are normally associated with mechanised locomotion and rails of iron or steel. Within the scope of this category are the Red Lake Railway (china clay) and the Rattlebrook peat railway. Tramways were, in general, the forerunners of the railways; their tracks were of metal, wood or stone, and traction was provided by methods in use before the introduction of steam engines (notably horses and gravity). A metal tramway served the naphtha works once in operation at Princetown. Its route can be followed from a gate in the prison enclosures on the north side of the road east of Rundlestone Corner, past Fice's Well to a loading wharf just beyond the last prison fence. South of the road the route of the track going towards the prison can be seen from outside the enclosures (access prohibited).

Further mention is made of railways and tramways in Part VII: Industry, in the sections on peat, china clay and granite.

Remains of bridge near Princetown

King Tor Halt

A derelict bridge, now restored for walkers, on the old Princetown Railway (582732), visible from the Two Bridges-Yelverton Road in the vicinity of Meavy Head.

At **King Tor Halt** (565732), the first stage in its course from Princetown, and 1½ miles from the station, the railway projected a branch line to Foggintor Quarries. From the halt the track describes a 2-mile loop around King's Tor and Swell Tor quarries, to repass 400 yards to the south-west, having lost 150 feet in height.

Bridges

In this wet hill-country bridges are a part of everyday life - essential but taken for granted. Obviously always utilitarian in concept and often doing nothing to enhance the view, there are places where a bridge fits so naturally into an enchanting landscape - Fingle, Norsworthy, Buckland, Saddle, Hisley, Huccaby - and there are many more.

River crossings start with fords, most of which are well-known reference points with familiar names. There may be stepping-stones (known as "steps"), consisting of either convenient naturally-occurring rocks, or a series of flat-topped boulders specially arranged for the purpose.

Because of the reasons mentioned earlier, stone has usually been preferred for bridges. However, there are a few wooden bridges, with designs ranging from small footbridges to those sufficiently robust to take vehicular traffic, but few are of any great aesthetic interest, apart from the charming locations in which they may be found. The old term "clam" for a wooden footbridge is still heard from time to time.

It is likely that there have been bridges at or near some of the present sites since at least medieval times, on the routes of old pack-horse tracks, but it is better to avoid the general term "medieval pack-horse bridge" for the primitive stone structures known as "clapper bridges". Storm water can have a disastrous effect, and historical evidence admits the repair of most of the larger ones in comparatively recent times.

I have illustrated several clappers, including the best-known of them (Postbridge). Others which can be seen easily (as they are adjacent to the highway) are those at Dartmeet and The Oakery. The remains of the Dartmeet clapper bridge (Forest/Widecombe, 672732) are immediately above the county bridge which carries the Ashburton-Two Bridges highway over the East Dart. It may originally have had as many as five spans. The Oakery (or Ockery) clapper (Forest, 594742) spans the Blackabrook between Two Bridges and Princetown.

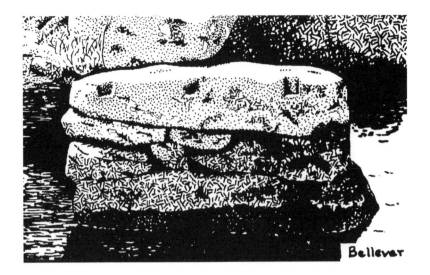

Bellever Clapper Bridge (Forest, 658773). It is thought that the missing central span may have been of wood, as there are sockets in the top stones of the relevant piers which might have accommodated supporting timbers.

◆

(illustrated overleaf)

A two-span clapper bridge which crosses the Cherry Brook at Powder Mills (Forest, 628771), north of the road between Postbridge and Two Bridges.

A single-stone clapper bridge, drowned by the flooding of the South Teign valley to create the reservoir at Fernworthy, and now only seen when the water level is low. (Forest, 662839.)

Clapper bridges over the Wheal Emma Leat. Single-span bridges of a variety of widths cross the leat as it traverses the moor south of the Swincombe.

Clapper Bridges

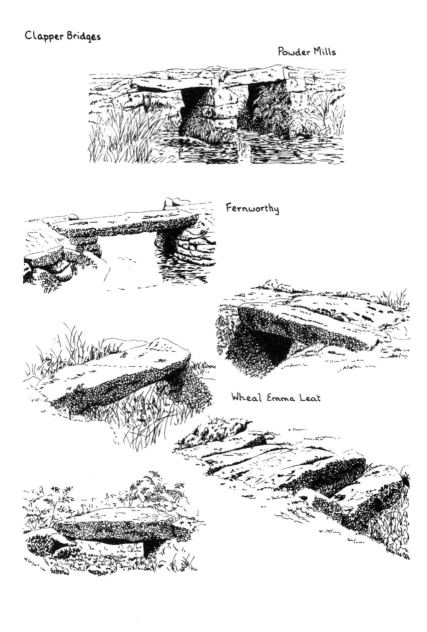

Powder Mills

Fernworthy

Wheal Emma Leat

(illustrated overleaf)

Teignever Clapper (OS Teign-e-ver invalid). The name is probably derived from Teignaford (Teign Ford). It spans the North Teign between Batworthy Corner and Scorhill (Gidleigh, 653870), above its confluence with Wallabrook (not below the confluence, as in Crossing's *Guide*).

Wallabrook Clapper (653871), a large single slab over the Wallabrook near Teignever Bridge.

Lether Tor Bridge (Walkhampton,569699), an improved clapper with parapets and a consolidated surface, crosses the Meavy 650 yards north of Norsworthy Bridge.

Swincombe Ford (Forest, 642725) opposite John Bishop's House, a not unusual arrangement where a ford is augmented by stepping stones and a bridge (in this case, as for example at High Down Ford, a wooden footbridge).

A sheep-leap over the Devonport Leat (Forest, 607705) below Whiteworks. Negotiating streams is usually no problem for stock, but crossing a wide leat with vertical sides and no conveniently-placed boulders in the channel can be a difficult matter. An occasional sheep-leap solves the problem. A stone projecting from each (or one) side reduces the length of the jump.

Teignhead Bridge (Forest, 639845) carries the track from Metheral and Fernworthy over the North Teign to Teignhead Farm, 400 yards WSW.

Postbridge Clapper (Forest, 648789), a restored three-span structure below the road bridge which carries the Moretonhampstead-Two Bridges road over the East Dart.

Beardown Clapper Bridge (Forest, 602753) crosses the Cowsic a short distance above the Beardown Farm road bridge, and is visible from the highway to the west of Two Bridges.

Huntingdon Clapper Bridge (Forest, 657662) spans the Avon below the southern slope of Huntingdon Warren. This is a case where comparative newness is confirmed by clear evidence of the feather-and-tare method used in splitting the slabs.

Teignever Bridge

Wallabrook clapper

Lether Tor Bridge

Fairy Bridge, Swincombe Steps and Ford

Sheep leap (Whiteworks)

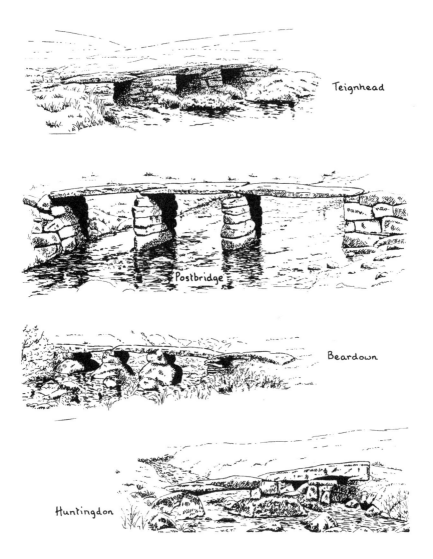

Teignhead

Postbridge

Beardown

Huntingdon

Hisley Bridge (Lustleigh, 780800), an early pack-horse bridge over the Bovey at the foot of Trendlebere Down).

Fernworthy Bridge (Forest, 663839) seen here during October 1971, one of the occasions when the reservoir level has been low, is on the road to Fernworthy Farm.

Bellever Bridge (Forest, 658773) crosses the East Dart at a popular location at the edge of Bellever Plantation. It carries the road which goes from Postbridge towards Cator, and overlooks the remains of the earlier clapper bridge.

Horrabridge. This structure, which crosses the Walkham within the village (513699), is possibly 14th century. In its parapet is a stone with an incised cross.

Huccaby (or **Hexworthy**) **Bridge** (Forest, 659729) carries the road from Holne to Hexworthy Cross, over the West Dart below the Forest Inn.

Fingle Bridge (Moretonhampstead/Drewsteignton, 743899) crosses the Teign in Fingle Gorge, with Prestonbury Castle, an Iron Age hill-fort, immediately above it to the east, and another such site, Cranbrook Castle, beyond the opposing hill to the SSW. Fingle Bridge is an example of a situation where the juxtaposition of road, river, access and spectacular scenery has made a popular location.

New Bridge (Holne/Widecombe, 711708), where the highway from Ashburton, on its way towards Dartmeet, crosses the Dart, is another focal point. Cutwaters, incorporated into the design of these structures, reduce the effect of the current and provide refuges for pedestrians.

Postbridge (Forest, 648789). The county bridge, which spans the East Dart between Moretonhampstead and Two Bridges, is seen here viewed from the nearby clapper bridge.

Nosworthy (or **Norsworthy**) **Bridge** (Walkhampton, 567693) over the Meavy near the head of Burrator reservoir.

Saddle Bridge (Forest/Holne, 664719) crosses O Brook between Hexworthy and Cumston Tor. Adjacent to the bridge is the site of a Pelton wheel, which used to supply electricity to the Hexworthy mines.

Pizwell Bridge (Forest/Widecombe, 669776) spans the Wallabrook (East Dart tributary) between Cator and Bellever.

Part VII
INDUSTRY

There must be "grey areas" between "habitual employment in useful work" (*Concise Oxford Dictionary*) as applied to cottage industry (or industry of a domestic nature) and industry on a commercial scale. The subjects I am about to touch upon tend generally towards the latter interpretation, and because so many signs of Dartmoor's industry relate to past activities they come for the most part under the accepted heading of "industrial archaeology".

Most of our present knowledge of this fascinating side of Dartmoor's history has been summarised in Helen Harris's indispensable book on the subject (4th ed. 1992).

Wool

The Devon wool trade, quite as relevant to Dartmoor in medieval times as was the tin industry, had its ups and downs, but in general continued to flourish long after the latter showed signs of decline, with local spinning and weaving being maintained at a considerable level until the upsurge of industry in the north of the country took effect in the 19th century.

A coarse serge was produced around medieval Dartmoor using a yarn obtained by working in lambswool and flock with the wool from Devon and Dartmoor sheep. Later improvements in breeds and admixture with finer wool brought a limited enhancement to the quality of the local cloth.

Some spinning and weaving was traditionally carried out as a cottage industry, but the main large-scale sites were in the border towns, where water from the Dartmoor streams provided power for the fulling- and tucking-mills. Most of those mill buildings which remain are now disused as such, and the long-established Dartmoor woollen industry now continues on a comparatively small scale.

Corn

From medieval times, when each manor had its own corn mill, until the advent of modern commercial milling, there were numerous corn or "grist" mills in the region. The mill which was important to central

Dartmoor was at Babeny (672751). The mill building is gone, and several which survive elsewhere are now used as dwelling-houses (e.g. at Cockingford and Bagtor) or for other purposes.

Abandoned millstones have been mentioned, but there is another sign of corn processing to be seen on the open moor. On Royal Hill (Forest, 616724), in the vicinity of a deserted site, are the remains of a "windstrew" or winnowing platform. There is another at Longstone (Sheepstor, 557684), within the boundary fence of Burrator Reservoir.

Peat

The peat bogs of the high moors are the product of the decomposition of vegetation under the ideal conditions of wet subsoil (which here is rotted granite in the form of either growan or china clay), damp atmosphere and low average temperatures. The relevance of peat to the Dartmoor story is illustrated by the extensive areas on the northern moors which show signs of large-scale digging.

There are a number of ruinous shelters associated with peat-cutting. They were generally small and simple, as exemplified by Will May's House (at the edge of the mire 1100 yards due east of the Thirlstone (Gidleigh, 639868) dating probably from the late 1700s), Stat's House on Marsh Hill (Forest, 621824), and Moute's Inn on Whitehorse Hill (Forest, 615850). (See Brian le Messurier in TDA 111, 1979.)

Being very water-retentive, difficult to dry and only about half as efficient as coal, the value of peat as a fuel has lain principally in its domestic use. It has played a part in industry, however, in various ways. It was used by the early tinners, to whom it was known as blackwood, and at some time they became aware of the value of its conversion to charcoal, which was capable of producing greater heat. The humped mounds or "meilers" and granite kilns associated with this process can be found in the vicinity of Wild Tor.

A lot of peat was dug in connection with the later period of shaft mining; it is well-known, for example, that peat was taken by pack-horse to the western edge of the moor from the area around Walkham Head. From this same locality (from Yearlick, or Greena, Ball) a tramway was constructed in 1846 to transport peat to the naphtha works at Princetown.

The Zeal Tor Tramroad (5ft gauge) brought peat from the ties at Red Lake to the naphtha works at Shipley Bridge for a short period from 1847 until about 1850. The rails were unusual in that they were made of wood and were bolted to individual granite blocks - there were no sleepers. Some of the stones are still to be seen with the bolts in situ. Some years later the tramroad was put into use again, this time in connection with a small china clay undertaking at Petre's Pits.

The peat industry on Dartmoor reached its zenith with the activities at Rattlebrook Head, dating from about 1868. A drying plant was set up there and peat was brought down by railway until the 1930s. Peat was still being brought down, however, by lorry, for horticultural use, about twenty years later.

A sunken track, seen here between Hunt's Tor and Gren (Grenny) Tor, by way of which peat was brought down over Bridestowe and Sourton Common from the vicinity of Kitty Tor on Amicombe Hill. 553878.

The remains of Bleak House (just within the Forest, 559865) on the left bank of the Rattlebrook between Green Tor and Higher Dunnagoat. The house, originally called Dunnagoat Cottage, was built for the manager of the Rattlebrook Peatworks.

Uncle Ab's House (South Brent, 656639), which was used probably for stabling horses, stands by an old track at the head of Middle Brook (Avon). The track (the Jobbers' Path) ran from Ball Gate, and connected with the track of the Zeal Tor tramway. It is thought that the building was used originally for pack-horses, and later for work-horses employed at the Zeal Tor undertaking. There is a stone near the house inscribed "CB 1809".

(illustrated overleaf)

Disintegration of blanket bog near Cranmere Pool (Forest, 6086). Fragmentation of the peat layer has occurred over an extensive area of the northern moor, resulting from accelerating erosion of drainage channels, and giving rise to "peat hags" separated by fissures several feet deep.

At **Broadamarsh,** where a Phillpotts peat pass descends over Winney's Down, there is a well-marked edge to the peat-dug area. (Forest, 6182.)

Rattlebrook Peatworks railway. The end of the track. In 1878 a standard-gauge railway was completed between the peatworks at Rattlebrook Head and the London and SW Railway at Bridestowe. At a point where a curve of sufficient radius could not be obtained a system of driving in and reversing out, over a set of points, was adopted. A narrow-gauge tramway connected the drying plant with the turf-ties on Amicombe Hill (in the background).

Old peat track
— Woodcock Hill

Bleak House

Uncle Ab's
House

Peat hags near Cranmere

The edge of the peat - Broadamarsh

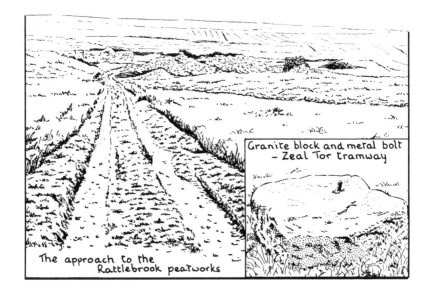

The approach to the Rattlebrook peatworks

Granite block and metal bolt - Zeal Tor tramway

Warrens

The rabbit was introduced to this country by the Normans for food and sport, and although it was subject to game laws for centuries, it became a major pest of agriculture. It is known to have existed on Dartmoor in the 12th century, and from medieval times was extensively farmed, in specially prepared warrens. The practice began in the south-western part of the moor, no doubt in parallel with the advent of tin-streaming in that area, and later spread to other parts.

The system involved enclosing a wide area of moorland - walls were built where there were no natural barriers - and making a number of artificial "buries" in which the rabbits bred. The warrener, who normally (though not always) lived in a house at the site, harvested the crop in the winter months and sold the meat either locally or in the border towns, and the skins to furriers. He used dogs and ferrets, the former being kept in an enclosure near the house. At Ditsworthy the kennels can be seen built into the walls of the kennel field, and at Trowlesworthy the dogs were provided with wooden barrels in a high-walled enclosure known as the "dog pit".

To deal with unwanted predators such as stoats, weasels and no doubt polecats, vermin traps were constructed, where the mustelids were known to have their runs. The traps were of one basic design, i.e. a granite box with a sliding door of slate at each end. "Funnel" walls were arranged so as to guide the creatures into the trap, and both slates would be dropped by means of a trip mechanism. There were variations of this design, depending, for example, on whether the traps were built into enclosure walls. The details of the trip mechanism and design variations are described and illustrated by Helen Harris (1992). Near the left bank of the Dart below Dartmeet there is a unique vermin-drowning trap.

The fortunes of the warrens fluctuated, in common with other Dartmoor enterprises, and the trade eventually ceased, although some warrens were operational well into the 20th century.

A bury or artificial burrow, one of the very many to be found in Dartmoor warrens. (The term "pillow mounds" has been revived on recent maps.)

A stone kennel, one of three at Ditsworthy, later superseded by cosier (and healthier) wooden accommodation.

A vermin trap at Legis Tor (Sheepstor, 571655). There are many vermin traps, in various stages of dilapidation (including those which have been vandalised).

The warren house at Ditsworthy. The warren (Sheepstor, 5866), the last to operate on Dartmoor, ceased to function commercially in the 1940s.

Early Tinning

Although there must have been a knowledge of tin-working in earlier times, there is no clear sign that tin was extracted on the moor until the latter half of the 12th century. It was then that rich stream deposits of cassiterite (tin ore), washed down to the lower levels, were discovered on the south-west side. This resulted in the first significant industrial upheaval to affect the moor.

Tinners' spoil-heaps are a common feature on the banks of most of the streams, activity having spread to other areas, and to higher reaches, where larger stone, not so easily carried by the current, would have been worked.

In the midst of the spoil-heaps are to be found the remains of tinners' huts, some of which can be recognised as processing sites (tinners' mills) by virtue of their design and by the relics of the operations by means of which the ore was reduced.

The tin-bearing stone would first be broken down by the use of a "pestle-and-mortar" system. The mortar stone started off with a fairly flat upper surface and developed a basin-shaped depression; when this became too deep the stone was discarded or turned over to present a new surface. It is not clear what was used as a pestle, but in more recent times banks of metal-bound wooden stamps were used, each set of stamps working over a multiple mortar. This apparatus was known as a knacking mill.

The mortar stones found at tinners' mills are usually single or double, but triple stones can be seen in at least four places (Venford, Gobbet, Beara and Norsworthy).

Evidence of another stage in the process, the use of a "crazing mill", is not so common, which suggests that it was not always necessary. A crazing mill, basically, followed a standard grinding-mill pattern - two circular stones, the upper stone being made to rotate over the lower one in order to reduce the ore to fine particles.

The term "blowing house" is reserved for those sites where it is known that smelting took place. Here the metal was extracted from the ore by means of a furnace, and was cast into ingots. The mould was shaped like an old traditional bread-tin, and there is sometimes, in the same block, a small sample mould.

To facilitate the operation of the machinery (no doubt earlier worked by man- or horse-power) water was brought to the site, by means of a leat, from an intake higher up the stream. In some of the ruins the remains of the wheel-pit can be identified.

The early affairs of the tinners of Devon and Cornwall were deliberated at Stannary Parliaments held on Hingston Down in Cornwall. At some time before 1305 the tinners of Devon separated from those of Cornwall. Tavistock, Ashburton and Chagford were appointed as Stannary Towns, to which all Devon tin was to be taken to be weighed and stamped. Plympton then replaced Tavistock, to be followed by Tavistock's reinstatement. Almost two centuries later (1494) there is the first record of a Parliament held on Crockern Tor - a location comparably accessible from the four towns. Naturally open air meetings at the top of a tor, held on successive days, could be uncomfortable at times, and later Parliaments opened on Crockern Tor and then adjourned to Tavistock.

Comprehensive records of tin production were kept from about the last decade of the 13th century, interrupted by the disastrous period of the Black Death, beginning about 1348, and new production maxima were achieved in the first half of the 16th century (subsequent to the end of what is generally regarded as the medieval period). The industry then declined, with no record of any tin being produced at the time of the Civil War.

The visual effects of extraction by the early methods reaches its peak in the spectacular upheavals at Erme Pits (Cornwood, 623668) - Crossing mentioned a kind of ore called zill tin being worked there in 1672.

After stream work had effectively ceased, the heavier processes of extraction from surface, and more particularly from subterranean lodes, were to wait for the introduction of more efficient methods.

(illustrated overleaf)

A tinners' hut (Forest, 629669) on the left bank of Blacklane Brook (Wollake). This is one of the many ruins associated with tin-working which show no sign of the apparatus involved in tin extraction. A proportion of them were no doubt dwellings occupied by tinners or stabling for their animals, and are quite likely to have been of a primitive nature. Not far from this particular ruin is the site of a tinners' mill which it is thought might be the Wollake Mill mentioned in a record of 1538.

A blowing house by the Walkham's right bank (Peter Tavy, 552766) a mile above Merrivale Bridge. The detail shown, of which the principal feature is the mould-stone, is from one of three blowing houses along this stretch of river.

A cave by Deancombe Brook (Sheepstor, 589685) to the south-east of Cuckoo Rock, probably used as a place of concealment by tinners. In the same locality there are other caches, including a beehive hut, and there is also a tinners' mill. A stone-lined chamber near the derelict site of Lether Tor Farm, Walkhampton (in the bank at the higher edge of Clam Meadow, 567697) is labelled "fogou" on the OS map. There is no clue to its age or use. The term "fogou" comes from the Cornish for cave, and was used by Cornish tinners for their places of concealment. (The term is also applied to the more pretentious underground passages of prehistoric and Roman times found on the Land's End peninsula.)

Beehive hut. There are quite a number of little structures called "beehive huts" or "tinners' caches". Their small size and low corbelled design would have restricted their use to storage, probably of tools or ingots of tin. The best-known example is this one by Lade Hill Brook (Forest, 639814), a tributary of the East Dart, above Postbridge. There is another, well-known but less easily seen, known as Downing's House, by the brook of that name, a little feeder of the Erme. Others have been described, and there have been reports of the discovery of previously unrecorded "possibles".

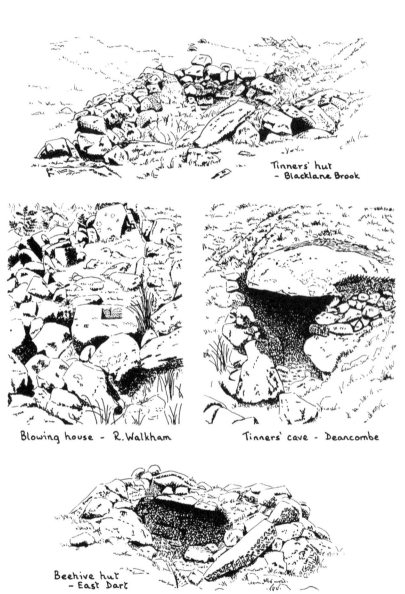

Tinners' hut
- Blacklane Brook

Blowing house - R. Walkham

Tinners' cave - Deancombe

Beehive hut
- East Dart

(illustrated overleaf)
Norsworthy left bank tinners' mill (Walkhampton, 567696) lies 250 yards north of Norsworthy Bridge, and below the track to Lether Tor Bridge. Among the numerous relics here, which include several mortars, are two stones which were no doubt used to accommodate axle bearings. One of the latter (on the right of the illustration) has a depression caused by rotational wear. There are also two stones with long slots, the purpose of which is not known. Another tinners' mill lies above the right bank 50 yards downstream, and can be found by following a wall which leaves the bank at right-angles. Nearby is a triple mortar-stone.

There is (or was) an unfinished mould-stone by the river 20 yards upstream from the bridge, which raises the question of whether smelting took place at either of these mills.

Lower blowing house, R.Walkham (Walkhampton, 552753) is sited 400 yards north of the road near Merrivale Bridge and 180 yards from the left bank. Among the remains which can be recognised here are the site of the furnace and a "float". The latter is a shallow granite trough designed to catch the molten metal.

Mould-stone, Higher Walkham blowing house (Peter Tavy, 552766). Having been collected in a float, the molten metal was transferred to a mould. In a corner of the block shown here is a small mould, a frequent feature of these stones, in which a specimen ingot was cast for assay purposes.

Tinners'
mill,
Nosworthy

Mortar
stones

Furnace
(Lower Walkham Blowing House)
Mould stone and float

Mould stone
(Higher Walkham Blowing House)

(illustrated overleaf)

Crazing-mill stones. Gobbet blowing house (Forest, 645728) lies alongside the waterworks road that runs above the right bank of the Swincombe. The site is special in that it is the only known place on Dartmoor where, in addition to mortar- and mould-stones, both stones of a crazing-mill are to be found. The upper stone is recognisable by the presence of additional, smaller, holes which accommodated the drive mechanism.

Detail at Black Tor Falls. 575716. There are two tinners' mills here, one either side of the Meavy, 200 yards south-east of Black Tor (Walkhampton), and 350 yards upstream from the Devonport Leat aqueduct. The doorway of the left bank building is intact, and the number XIII (perhaps the identification number of the mill) is incised in the lintel).

The "Blacksmiths' Shop" on the left bank of the Teign (Forest, 638842) above the outfall of Manga Brook, is more likely to have been a blowing house in spite of its name. There are mould-stones here, including two which are double. One of them is broken and the detached segment lies on the wall near the river. (There are other sites known as "The Blacksmiths' Shop", one of them being located in Beckamoor Combe (Whitchurch) - see page 269, where the presence of a wheelwrights' stone admits the validity of the name.)

A triple mortar, from the site of a blowing house now submerged by Venford reservoir, lies within the fence near the dam (Holne, 686712) across the road from the west car park.

Lower stone

Upper stone

Swincombe Blowing House
- crazing-mill stones

Black Tor Falls - detail of lintel

Block with trough
- broken through a second trough

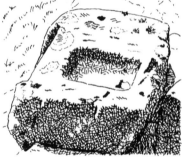

"The Blacksmith's Shop"(N.Teign)
Block with two troughs

Broken trough

(illustrated overleaf)

Parliament Rock (Forest, 616757). The tinners' parliament set itself apart from the Parliament in Westminster. The Stannaries were under the jurisdiction of the Crown but they had their own strict laws and harsh penalties, using the castle at Lydford as their prison. The deliberations of the stannators or jurats - twenty-four from each of the Stannary Towns - at Crockern Tor, are said to have been conducted from a natural seat on a pillar known as Parliament Rock.

Table and benches, Crockern Tor. With a little imagination one can interpret some of the rocks near Parliament Rock as the tables and benches at which the elected representatives sat.

The Judge's Table (Forest, 642742). Crossing gave an account of the supposed circumstances relating to the removal of the table and seats, and there is a tradition that the Judge's Table, the roofing stone of a well at Dunnabridge Farm, came from Crockern Tor.

Tinners' Rabbits. A design consisting of three rabbits with only three ears between them is to be seen on roof bosses in several churches in the Dartmoor country - Bridford, Chagford, Ilsington, North Bovey, Sampford Courtenay, South Tawton, Spreyton, Tavistock and Widecombe. The popular belief is that it was an ancient fertility symbol which found its way into Christianity as one of the several devices representing the Holy Trinity, and which was adopted by the Dartmoor medieval tinners as their special emblem.

Tom Greeves debates these points in DM (Winter 1991), suggesting that the name "Tinners' Rabbits" may be of comparatively recent origin, and discusses, in particular, whether these creatures are properly hares.

Parliament Rock
— Crockern Tor

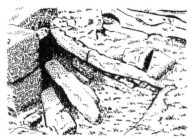

Table and benches – Crockern Tor

The Judge's Table – Dunnabridge Farm

Tinners'
Rabbits – Widecombe Church

Mining

Following a couple of centuries of low activity, during which there were token ventures into open-cast and shaft mining, the advent of more advanced technology, towards the end of the eighteenth century, brought a new generation of prospectors. With the introduction of deep mining they were able to tackle hitherto inaccessible lodes, and whilst tin remained almost the sole metalliferous product of the granite area the speculators also took an interest in extracting other minerals from the metamorphic aureole.

It was not now normal to carry out the smelting process on the moor, although there is a record of a smelting-house at "Ailsborough in Sheepstor" in 1826. Hemery (1983a) recorded that it was built in 1822. Worth wrote of the ruin at the head of Drizzlecombe: "This was the last tin-smelting place on Dartmoor, and cannot claim undoubted status as a blowing-house, since the furnace was possibly of the reverberatory type. Loss of tin in flue dust was evidently recognised, and a flue, over 70ft in length, was constructed".

New features of industrial archaeology now present themselves, such as the deep tinning gullies which scar the hillsides opposite the Warren House Inn, the yawning mouths of subterranean workings and the circular depressions representing the heads of infilled vertical shafts.

Water was still a very relevant factor and there were two fundamental problems - too much in the wrong place or too little where it was needed. Where adits (tunnels) were driven up into the hillsides waste water could run freely out of the workings, but where depth and angle of levels precluded the use of gravity, it had to be lifted. Leats were constructed, some several miles in length, and great wheels were erected to provide power, to shift not only water, but men and ore. As regards the problem of providing power where water could not be persuaded to flow, there was an ingenious system, the relics of which can be seen at the Eylesbarrow Mine. The motion produced at a water-wheel was transferred over a considerable distance by means of a long series of connected reciprocating rods to the site where power was needed. The rods worked back and forth on bearers supported by pairs of low stone pillars.

Although it was not now normal practice to extract the metal at the site, the ore was refined there by crushing in stamping mills and washing in buddles. Helen Harris reproduced illustrations of stamping mills, photographed in about 1887 and 1928. A common form of buddle is a large circular trough with rotating arms pivoted at a central boss. The lighter gravel, low in metal content, agitated by sacking attacked to the arms, was washed out, leaving behind the heavier particles which were rich in metal. Buddles can be seen at various sites; there are, for example, two large ones at Hooten Wheals, Hexworthy, below the site of the stamping mills, two smaller ones at the Golden Dagger Mine, two at Foxholes beyond Bra Tor, and three at West Vitifer.

At some mines water remained the only source of power, apart from that provided by men and animals, but with the introduction of the steam engine much greater efficiency was achieved at a number of mines. One of the last remaining engine-houses, that at Wheal Betsy, near the road at Mary Tavy, was taken into care.

The viability of tin mining fluctuated with changes in demand, price and recoverability, an important factor in its decline being the availability of cheaper Malayan tin.

Among the various minerals extracted from the metamorphic aureole, in addition to tin, were copper, lead, zinc and iron. A little silver was found in association with lead; and arsenic, apart from being mined in the form of mispickel (arsenical pyrites, $FeAsS$) was also obtained as a by-product of calcining (roasting) tin or copper ore in a further refining process. In fact, the arsenic so obtained was later to prove of greater value than the tin or copper.

With the first half of the twentieth century tungsten ore (wolfram) was being worked at Hemerdon Ball, and there was a mine producing barytes at Bridford. (There has also been mention of gold and uranium.)

Drizzlecombe smelting house (Sheepstor, 591676) is associated with the complex of remains at Eylesbarrow, and lies to the south of the mine track where a path comes up from Ditsworthy Warren. There is some substantial masonry here.

Flue at Drizzlecombe Blowing House (Eylesbarrow Mine)

Open shaft - Eylesbarrow   Flat rod system - Eylesbarrow

Open mine shaft. Among the signs of underground workings are the disused shafts which are frequent in the mining areas. Some were open, but are now sealed off.

Paired pillars at Eylesbarrow, 5968, evidence of a "flat rod system" for transmitting power. (Flat refers to the system, not the rods.)

A mine house. Foxholes Mine (Lydford, 546854) is by Doe Tor Brook 700 yards ESE of Widgery Cross. Among the remains here are the walls of the mine house and two buddles.

Middle Brook Old Wheelhouse (South Brent, 662635), which is associated with the tin-workings in the valley of this tributary of Bala Brook, is a conspicuous feature in a relatively featureless landscape to the west of Shipley Bridge.

A launder bank. It was generally necessary to build a launder or trough to direct water from a leat on to a wheel. The bank which was built to support the launder can often be distinguished among mine-workings, in association with a wheel pit.

A buddle in the valley of Redwater Brook (Manaton, 684800), to the east of the Warren House Inn.

───────────── ◆ ─────────────

(illustrated overleaf)
Druid Mine (Ashburton, 754715), the remains of which are near the road midway between Welstor Cross and Rewdon Cross, was worked during the mid-19th century, it is thought for copper (output unknown).

Wheal Betsy, in the valley of Cholwell Brook, was worked mainly for lead and its associated product silver, and ceased operations in 1877. The engine house and stack are near the highway at 510814 (Mary Tavy).

Hexworthy Mines, in the valley of O Brook, include Hensroost Mine (660710) and Hooten Wheals (655708). The mines were last worked in the early years of the 20th century, when electricity, generated at Saddle bridge, was used here. (Forest.)

Mine house
– Foxholes
Mine

Wheelhouse
– Middle Brook

Launder bank
– Foxholes
Mine

Buddle –
Golden Dagger
Mine

W.G.T.

Engine house,
Wheal Betsy,
Mary Tavy

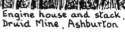

Engine house and stack,
Druid Mine, Ashburton

Remains of dressing floors,
Hooten Wheals, Hexworthy

An adit at South Devon United Mine (Peter Tavy, 511785). Further up the valley there is a Pelton wheel, and the remains of the plant used for producing arsenic. Perkins (1972) describes the process, with diagrams.

Adit – Peter Tavy

Golden Dagger

Golden Dagger Mine. The remains of the machinery bases in the valley of Redwater Brook (Manaton, 684800), within the conifer plantation (Soussons Down) south of Birch Tor and Vitifer Mines. Details of the machinery, with a plan, are given in an article by P.H.G. Richardson in DM No.17 (Winter 1989).

Bush Down. There are two large worked blocks lying a short distance north-east of King's Oven (Chagford, 675812). Their purpose is not known, but they may have had some connection with the Bush Down tin mine. The history of King's Oven (traditionally "Furnum Regis") is not clear, but it is thought to have

Slotted stones - Bush Down

had tin-smelting connections. Its site can be found by following a boundary hedge, as it curves up the hillside opposite the head of the Vitifer Mine track.

Granite

The utilisation of moorstone began with its application by prehistoric people to build the walls of their huts, their stock pens and enclosed settlements, and to raise their sacred circles, stone rows and cairns.

Surface stone has always been fairly readily available, particularly in the rock fields or clitter, but there came a time when it was expedient to split up larger rocks. Up to about 1800 a system known as the wedge-and-groove method was used. A series of slots was cut on the line of the intended separation, and the stone was split by driving in wedges (probably left to expand by frost action).

A row of semi-cylindrical notches along the edge of a stone is an indication of the feather-and-tare method used after that date. A series of holes is made with a jumper or similar tool, and in each hole a tare (tapered metal spike) is wedged between two packing pieces or "feathers", positioned so as to exert pressure in the required directions when the tares are struck. Stones split in this way are a common sight, and in the area to the west of Princetown there are signs of intensive working of surface stone. On the slopes of Staple Tor, for example, there are the relics of the work which was going on there in the latter part of the 19th century - sett-makers' bankers, the remains of workers' shelters, and numerous abandoned split stones and heaps of granite chippings.

Quarrying for granite had begun about a century before this, in about 1780, when Princetown was being developed and the roads across the moor were being made.

To the south-east of Merrivale are some of the best-known of the disused quarries - Foggintor, Little King Tor, Swell Tor and Ingra Tor, all served by the old Princetown railway. Foggintor is the easiest of these to approach (on foot) by way of the Yellowmead Farm track, which leaves the Tavistock-Two Bridges road opposite the site of the Mission Room (567750).

Turning to Haytor Down, there are five quarries distributed over a wide area (7577, etc) between Haytor Rocks and Houndtor Combe, extending westward to Holwell Tor and Emsworthy Rocks. The main period of operations here, beginning in 1828, lasted about forty years.

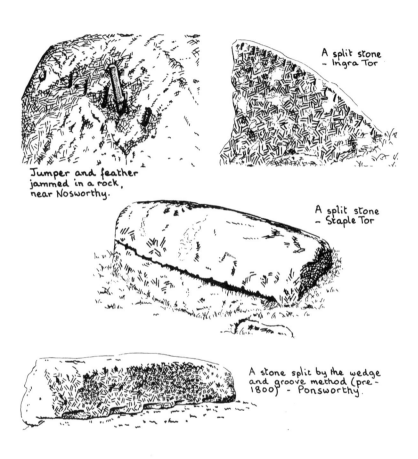

Jumper and feather jammed in a rock, near Nosworthy.

A split stone – Ingra Tor

A split stone – Staple Tor

A stone split by the wedge and groove method (pre-1800) – Ponsworthy.

Stone splitting method. Evidence of stone splitting by the feather-and-tare method is a common sight. The signs of the earlier wedge-and-groove method are not so obvious, but can often be detected on closer inspection of things like gateposts and lintels.

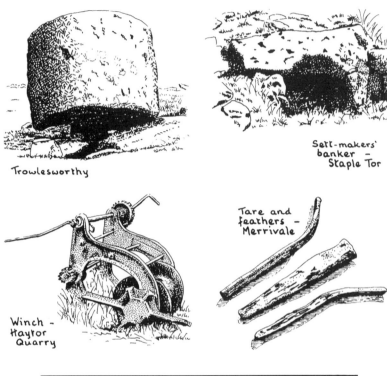

Trowlesworthy

Sett-makers'
banker –
Staple Tor

Winch –
Haytor
Quarry

Tare and
feathers –
Merrivale

Crane bases –
Ingra Tor

The 8½ mile Haytor Granite Tramway was built to facilitate the movement of stone to Teigngrace (from whence it was carried by barge, by way of the Stover Canal and Teign estuary to Teignmouth docks). The track was constructed from grooved or rebated setts, by means of which the unflanged wheels of the trucks were guided. There is a complex system of sidings, and the points, being made of granite, were immovable, the trucks being made to take the required route by the use of metal deflectors.

In addition to the major sites there are numerous small quarries, often at roadsides.

Merrivale Quarry (Whitchurch, 546752), alongside the highway between Tavistock and Two Bridges, is now the only operational granite quarry on the moor. Here massive blocks are lifted from an excavation of considerable depth, and shaped using a variety of mechanised techniques, including an endless saw which spans part of the site, but the old feather-and-tare method is still in use.

A massive cylindrical block at Trowlesworthy Tors (Shaugh Prior, 578644), intended as the base of a flag-pole for Devonport, but abandoned where it had been cut.

A sett-makers' banker on the south-east slope of Great Staple Tor (Whitchurch, 543759), one of a number in this area - stone benches where the granite was split into "setts" or blocks, for road building.

A winch at Haytor, lying derelict in one of the quarries, a sign of the thriving industry that was carried on there.

Tare and feathers seen at Merrivale Quarry.

Crane bases at Ingra Tor Quarry (Walkhampton, 555721), alongside the old Princetown Railway a mile to the north of Peek Hill Pond.

Deserted dwelling
- Foggintor

Worked granite
blocks - Swell Tor

Milestone - Colehayes

Quarry workers' shelter - Holwell

Foggintor Quarry (Walkhampton, 566736). The name of the quarry suggests that there was a tor here; if there wás, it has disappeared in the process of quarrying, and a large water-filled excavation has taken its place. There are several ruinous buildings.

Swell Tor Quarry, a short distance WSW (560733). The carved blocks are corbels, designed to support the flying walkways of London Bridge, and surplus to the original requirements. Replacements were taken from here when the bridge was moved to America.

A milestone by the Haytor granite tramway, where it passes through Colehayes Plantation (private). Bovey Tracey, 799781.

Quarry workers' shelter (Ilsington, 750777). A diminutive man-made cave near the terminus of the Holwell Quarry branch of the Haytor tramway, overlooking Houndtor Combe.

Haytor Granite Tramway. A set of points constructed, as was the whole of this complex tramway system, from granite blocks. The hole in the sett at left centre indicates the position of a movable iron deflector. (Ilsington, 762777.)

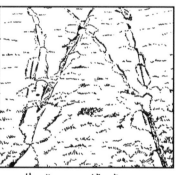

Haytor granite tramway

Stone-workers' jumper

The tool jammed in a rock near Norsworthy (see page 217) was of a type associated with pneumatic drilling, and so bore little resemblance to the hand-operated jumper illustrated here. This tool was about four feet long, sharpened at each end and weighted at the centre. Simon Butler (1986) reproduced an old photograph of the prison quarry at Princetown, showing these jumpers in use.

China Clay

During the cooling process which followed the formation of the granite the attack of solutions and vapours from beneath caused the felspar in some areas to soften into clay (kaolinisation) whilst leaving the quartz and mica unchanged. This was a gradual upward process which created very deep and extensive deposits of china clay or kaolin such as those on the south-western fringe of the National Park.

China clay derived its name from its use in ceramics, mainly in China, but it is also associated with a variety of other industries including paper, paint, plastics, textiles and pharmaceuticals.

The most notable of the abandoned clay undertakings is at Red Lake, where the conical spoil-heap stands conspicuously in the heart of the southern moor. A railway was constructed between Red Lake and Bittaford, a distance of $7\frac{1}{2}$ miles, to transport men and equipment by steam train. By contouring the hillsides in order to maintain a fairly uniform gradient, the route was far from straight. The rails are gone, but the well-marked track remains, which facilitates access (on foot) to a remote part of the moor.

After the waste had been separated out the clay came down in suspension by gravity pipeline and was recovered at the Cantrell works. There are the remains of settling tanks at Crossways and at the smaller clay pit at Left Lake. Associated relics at the Bittaford end include the engine shed (on private land); the drying sheds are now an engineering works.

The Zeal Tor wooden tramway, laid down to transport peat from Red Lake, was put into use again in connection with a small china clay undertaking at Petre's Pits (at Bala Brook Head), and a branch, apparently with iron rails, was constructed. Like the Red Lake railway it would have carried men and equipment. The clay was delivered, suspended in water, by means of a leat, to the settling tanks at Shipley Bridge. The final stage of settlement is represented by the derelict building which stands at the rear of the car park. From here the suspension, of a "porridgey" consistency, was delivered through the chutes in the wall to the drying pans situated on the car park site. The main complex of settling and holding tanks is located on the hillside to the rear. At one time there were some tip-trucks to be seen by the branch to Petre's Pits, indicating that some material, perhaps waste, was shifted there. Like the earlier naphtha project in this area, this enterprise also failed.

China clay -
The Red Lake workings

Spoil heap at
Red Lake

The spoil-heap at Red Lake (Forest, 646669) stands in conspicuous isolation beside the water-filled clay-pit.

Pipeline conduit

The china clay pipeline bridging a gully alongside the Red Lake Railway.

The old railway track
passing Left Lake clay works

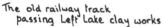

Left Lake clay works (Harford/Ugborough). The spoil-heap and remains of the track-side installation. 646634.

Settling tanks at Crossways. There are several derelict tanks in this area at the northern tip of Ugborough parish. (650666)

Clay pit, Lee Moor (Shaugh Prior), viewed from approximately 570629, as it was in 1966.

The advanced state of decomposition of the felspar in the Lee Moor area has enabled it to be used, among other applications, for the manufacture of high-quality ceramics. Among the less-refined products originating there were the building bricks marked "Martin Leemoor" which can be seen on the moor (e.g. at the derelict site of Kingsett Farm, 577699). There has been a very limited use for the colossal quantities of waste (eight times the weight of the kaolin extracted) because of high transport costs. Thus the spoil-heaps are a significant feature of the landscape of china clay country.

From the earliest days of china clay working a reliable water supply has been essential. To serve the Lee Moor workings a 4-mile leat was constructed to take water from the Plym near Ditsworthy Warren.

A tramway was initiated in 1858; at its greatest extent it ran from the Cholwich Town works, and after being joined by the Wotter tramway, it went by way of Cann Wood to Martin's (Laira) Wharf on the Plym estuary, where the clay schooners docked. There were two cable inclines where trucks descended by gravity, counterbalanced by trucks going up loaded with materials needed at the workings. Steam traction was introduced to part of the route in 1899, but the use of the track ceased in stages. From 1940 transport was by lorry, and from 1947 by pipeline to the Marsh Mills drying plant ($5\frac{1}{2}$ miles).

In the modern process used at this site the clay is washed out by high-pressure water-jets (or "monitors"). The resultant slurry is passed through a rectangular tank where the heavy "sand", which sinks to the bottom, is lifted out by a bucket wheel, and transported to spoil-heaps by dumper lorry. The lighter material, in suspension, goes through mica separation, de-watering and further refining processes before drying.

Clay extraction is still actively proceeding at Lee Moor; it has involved the closure of the road from Tolchmoor Gate towards Cadover Bridge, and threatens to penetrate deep into the National Park.

The Powder Mills

The remains of the Powder Mills are a short distance from the Moretonhampstead-Two Bridges road opposite Bellever Plantation. Though confined to one small area (Forest, 6277) they are a unique and significant feature of central Dartmoor.

Rock- or black powder was once much in local demand, in the tin-mining and granite industries for blasting purposes. Manufacture took place here from 1844 until nearly 1900, the cessation of operations following the invention of dynamite.

Proving mortar

A mortar, standing by the approach road to the site, was used for batch testing.

Broken millstone

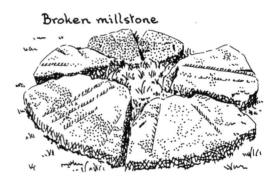

Millstones at this site were made, not of granite, but of hard border rock, in the interests of safe and efficient grinding.

Pair of mill buildings

The Powder Mills. Though the walls are of very solid construction the roofs were comparatively flimsy to minimise the consequences of accidental explosion.

Wheel housing and leat. Each wheel served a pair of mills. Water taken from the East Dart 1½ miles above Postbridge was used in an ingenious distribution system, and ultimately discharged into the Cherry Brook. Manipulation of the water flow for working the mills contributed to the marshy nature of the ground on the course of the Lich Way between the mills and the highway.

Wheel housing and leat

_____ Other Industrial Sites _____

Interesting not only in its singular application but also in that it is a feature of the open moor, is a site associated with a project to supply ice, produced by harnessing natural processes, to the fishing industry of the South-West. The ice could be stored underground at the site well into the warmer months, but in view of a reversal of the same natural processes during the lengthy periods involved in delivery, the business only lasted three years. The site is a short distance north-east of Sourton Tors (546901).

Ball clay, a drift deposit originating from the china clay of Dartmoor and currently being worked in the Bovey Basin, was once obtained for use at a pottery at Bovey Tracey from Bovey Heath and from the pit at Bluewaters (810770 approx., on private land). Three bottle kilns still stand at the pottery site (815772).

An ambitious project to exploit the lignite deposits in the same area, involving German industrialists, was short-lived owing to the outbreak of the 1914 war. (Lignite or brown coal is intermediate between peat and humic coal.) (Tregonning, 1983).

There have been numerous other industries in the Dartmoor area, with or without strictly moorland connotations, including the paper mill at Ivybridge (still in operation), the brickworks at Horrabridge, the umber works and marble works at Ashburton, the granulite quarry and glassworks at Meldon, and so on. The Finch Foundry, an edge-tool mill at Sticklepath, is of particular interest as it has been restored to working order, and is now a museum.

Many of the hides from Dartmoor stock were no doubt processed at the local tanneries, of which there were several in the border towns, and oak bark obtained from the fringe woodlands was used in this connection. The Sticklepath tannery had an associated candle factory.

The natural vegetation of the moor has been used in various ways, for example the harvesting of whortleberries for sale was once carried out at a sufficiently high level to be classed as a minor industry .

Part VIII
WAYSIDE STONES AND BOUNDARY MARKS

The wayside stones of Devon, and of Dartmoor in particular, have been the subject of research for many years, especially by the late E.N.Masson Phillips, whose results were published periodically in TDA, and there are specialised books on at least two of the categories - stone crosses and boundary markers. Many of them are indicated on the OS maps at the popular scale of 1:25000, and I find the Dartmoor maps at 6 inches to the mile an invaluable source of information. The features marked thereon as "BS" or "Stone" are often worth investigating, and can open up new avenues of enquiry. The convenience of wayside stones for survey work is illustrated by the frequency of bench marks upon them.

The"**Venville Stone**", built into a wall on the south side of Quarry Lane, near Moortown, Whitchurch (523738). In Crossing's *Guide* it is described as a Blowing Stone, formerly used to amplify the sound of the horn when summoning those whose duty it was to assist in driving (stock from) the moor .

Stone Crosses

The ancient stone crosses of Dartmoor are known to have served a variety of purposes. There were village or preaching crosses, and those set up by the wayside as route markers and perhaps as shrines. Some were adopted as boundary marks, though whether any were established specifically for the purpose is not clear (apart from a few small cruciform incisions on boulders or posts).

Nun's Cross, $2\frac{1}{4}$ miles SSE of Princetown, is the most celebrated of the large free-standing crosses; it is known to have been in existence in the year 1240, having been used as a Forest bondmark. Another cross of great antiquity - at Sourton Down - was apparently shaped as a cross from a Celtic memorial stone of the 5th or 6th century.

The design of the crosses, though in general fairly basic, is very variable, and in many cases there may be an incised cross or a cross in relief on one or both faces.

Some of the crosses are in relatively good condition, and a lot of them have been repaired or rebuilt; others are fragmentary. A considerable number of them are known to have been moved, or used for other purposes, particularly as gateposts.

The subject has been covered in great detail by William Crossing (1902), E.N. Masson Phillips in TDA, and Harry Starkey (1983). My main purpose is to bring together illustrations of the majority of the older crosses.

The first three drawings illustrate the limits of the range of subjects which may justifiably be included under the heading of "stone crosses". Childe's Tomb is a substantial structure where a comparatively new cross (replacing an old one) has been erected over a prehistoric burial site, It stands in a remote situation. At the other extreme are (i) a fragment of a socket-stone and (ii) merely a cruciform incision on a stone slab, but obviously very old, at a little village church.

Near
Childe's Tomb

Childe's Tomb (Forest, 626703), north of Fox Tor, is a modern cross set on a base of large stone blocks, over a kistvaen. Part of the socket-stone of an earlier cross lies nearby. The site derives its name from the legend of Childe the Hunter of Plymstock.

An incised cross forming part of the pattern on a grave-cover or "coffin lid" which leans against the wall of Belstone church. Crossing recorded that it was found in 1861 when some steps leading to the vestry were being taken down. (See also Harry Starkey 1986 and John Chudleigh 1893.)

Belstone

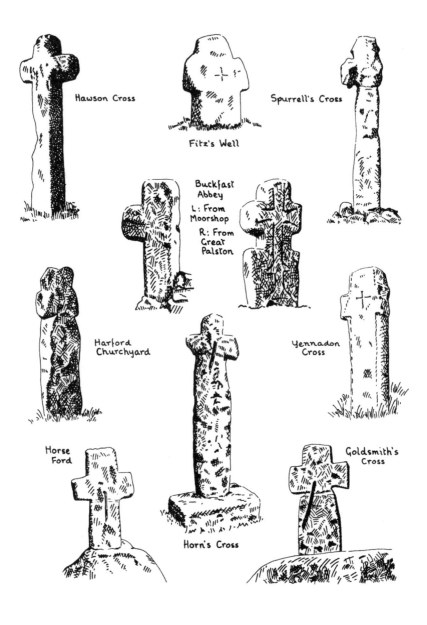

Hawson Cross

Fitz's Well

Spurrell's Cross

Buckfast Abbey
L: From Moorshop
R: From Great Palston

Harford Churchyard

Yennadon Cross

Horse Ford

Horn's Cross

Goldsmith's Cross

Hawson Cross (Buckfastleigh, 711682), at Stumpy Oak Crossroads, was moved from Hawson to its present position in 1952.

Fitz's Well (Okehampton, 592938). The cross stands by the road from the town to the moor gate.

Spurrell's Cross (Ugborough, 659599) consists of an ancient head of pinitic granite, with one arm missing, on a modern shaft; its spurred limbs are unique on Dartmoor. (There is a cross of similar age and design in Ermington church porch.)

Crosses at Buckfast Abbey (741693), near the site of the old main gate. One, a cross of unusual design, with an incised cruciform pattern on each face was previously at the entrance to **Great Palston Farm,** South Brent. The other was moved from **Moorshop,** Whitchurch, during the second world war.

Cross in Harford churchyard (638594), previously used as a gatepost.

Horn's Cross (Holne, 670710) stands on Holne Moor, 1/2 mile south of Cumston Tor.

Yennadon Cross (Walkhampton, 545694) was moved to this site (probably its original location) on 24th July 1974, having been previously in use (inverted) as a gatepost at Peekhill Farm.

Horse Ford Cross (Forest, 660713) is by the Hexworthy Mine track, above the valley of O Brook.

Goldsmith's Cross (Forest, 616701), on a large rock south of Foxtor Mires and east of Wheal Anne Bottom, was repaired minus the centre section of the shaft.

Burham (Walkhampton, 540691). A socket-stone at the entrance is possibly from Yennadon Cross (see above).

Dousland

A cross at Buckfastleigh, in the north-east corner of the churchyard. 742665.

Bennet's Cross (Chagford/North Bovey, 680817). (Hemery records that Benet is correct.) The cross, which stands on the south side of the Moretonhampsted-Two Bridges road, ½ mile north-east of the Warren House Inn, is inscribed WB (see Boundary stones).

Blackaton Cross (Shaugh Prior, 571631), consisting of an ancient head on a modern shaft, is alongside the old road through Lee Moor clay works (approachable from the Cadover Bridge direction).

Cross at Bickleigh (520625), on the green outside the churchyard. There is a modern shaft, but the pedestal and head are ancient. The crockets in the angles of the cross are unique in Devon.

Cross near Cadover Bridge (Meavy, 553647), on the slope 200 yards north-west of the bridge.

Crazywell Cross (Walkhampton, 584704), east of Crazywell Pool. An ancient head on a modern shaft.

Cross Gate Cross (Walkhampton, 562695), is at a road junction north of Burrator Reservoir. The head is incomplete - only the arms remain, mounted on a modern shaft, and set on an ancient pedestal.

Bovey Stone (Bovey Tracey, 814788), is built into the wall of Cross Cottage, by the Moretonhampstead road opposite Furzeleigh Lane, and consists of a socket-stone and part of a shaft with an incised cross. It formerly stood at Atway.

Cross at Cholwich Town (Cornwood, 586612). The shaft of a cross was moved from the farm in 1969 and was erected at the roadside by the farm entrance. It was stolen from there in 1978.

Hobajon's Cross (Harford/Ugborough, 655605), a small pillar with an incised cross, is in a prehistoric stone row on the parish boundary. The name was at one time erroneously applied to a cross on Three Barrows (see page 256).

Buckfastleigh
Churchyard

Bennett's Cross

Blackaton Cross

Cadover Bridge

Bickleigh

Classenwell Pool

Cross Gate

Cholwich Town

Cross Cottage

Hobajons Cross

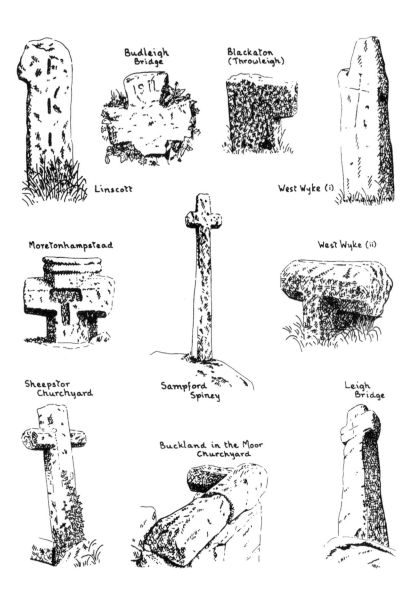

Linscott

Budleigh
Bridge

Blackaton
(Throwleigh)

West Wyke (i)

Moretonhampstead

West Wyke (ii)

Sheepstor
Churchyard

Sampford
Spiney

Leigh
Bridge

Buckland in the Moor
Churchyard

Cross at Linscott (Moretonhampstead, 741872). On the slope by a field gate near Linscott Cottages, it bears the recesses of a slotted gatepost.

Cross in Budleigh Bridge (Moretonhampstead, 762854). The head of a cross, apparently cut later than 1800, and with an incised date (1911), built into the parapet.

Cross at Blackaton (Throwleigh, 678890). Opposite the entrance, part of a cross with an incised cross within a circle on its visible face.

Crosses at West Wyke (West Week) (South Tawton, 657926). One is an inverted cross-head (not a "Tau" cross which, apart from heraldry, seems to be a figment of the antiquarian imagination) leaning against a tree-trunk at the farm entrance. The other, presenting a more normal appearance, though damaged, bears an incised cross, and stands nearby.

Cross at Moretonhampstead (755860). Another inverted cross-head, standing at the Cross Tree by the south entrance of the churchyard.

Cross at Sampford Spiney (534724), on the green near the church.

Cross in Sheepstor churchyard (560676), at the top of the steps south of the church; an octagonal shaft, fitted at some time with new arms.

Cross at Buckland in the Moor (720731). Fragments on the wall by the south gate of the churchyard.

Cross near Leigh Bridge (Chagford, 683876), on the wooded slope above the road from Holystreet. It may have come from Teigncombe, where there is a socket-stone.

Teigncombe

Teigncombe Farm (Chagford, 674871). The socket-stone referred to above is at a gateway near the farm.

Crosses on Whitchurch Down. (a) **Pixie's Cross** (501737), on the golf course, 1 mile north-east of Whitchurch, a large cross of peculiar shape. (b) West of the golf course, a cross consisting of an ancient head and socket-stone with a very short modern shaft. (493738.)

Hele Cross (North Bovey, 721841), at a road junction at Hele, ½ mile east of The Watching Place (page 248).

Nun's (or **Siward's**) **Cross** (Forest/Walkhampton, 605699), 2 ½ miles SSE of Princetown, is known to have been in existence in 1240. Inscribed BOC LOND, SIWARD (or SYWARD).

Ouldsbroom Cross (Widecombe, 685735). (Alternatively Ollsbrim, Ollsbroom.) The cross, which stands by the Ashburton-Two Bridges road a mile east of Dartmeet, was re-erected here, having been used as a gatepost at Lower Town Farm, Leusdon.

Cross on Rippon Tor (Ilsington, 747756). There is a recumbent cross carved in relief on the north-west side near the summit. Mr. Masson Phillips considered that it is an unfinished cross, abandoned before completion, like the millstone nearby. In lighter vein, I have heard it suggested that it may have been a stone "doodle" (a bit of light "relief") executed by someone who should have been more gainfully employed in fashioning millstones; and there have been other equally improbable ideas. Mike Barber, National Park ranger, told me of an incised cross among the summit rocks.

Cross at Sanduck Farm (Lustleigh, 768836). A restored cross at the roadside.

Cross at North Bovey (740839). A cross, with an unrelated socket-stone, stands on the village green. Part of what may be the original cross is preserved in a nearby cottage.

Cross at Truelove (Shaugh Prior, 550606). Between two gates at the top of the steep incline above the farmhouse, the head of a cross at the base of the hedge.

Pixie's
Cross
(Whitchurch
Down)

Hele

Nuns Cross

Whitchurch
Down

Ollsbroom

Rippon
Tor

Sanduck
Farm

North
Bovey

Truelove

Huntingdon Cross

Cross Gate (Drywell)

Coxtor Gate

Skir Ford

Manaton

Southcott

South Harton

Marchant's Cross

Okehampton

Ringhall

Huntingdon Cross (Forest, 664661), on the "Abbot's Way", above the confluence of Wester Wella Brook and the Avon.

Cross near Drywell (Widecombe, 701753). A cross at the crossroads between Jordan and Dockwell, reconstructed with a shaft brought from Totnes.

Skir (Skaur) Ford Cross (Forest, 654714), on Down Ridge, north of the Hexworthy Mines.

Cross at Coxtor Gate (Peter Tavy, 516761). A cross by the road to Coxtor Farm, used as a gatepost.

Cross in Manaton churchyard (749813). The earlier churchyard cross is missing. The socket-stone which presumably supported it now carries a substitute cross, found nearby.

Cross at Southcott (Okehampton, 550948). At Southcott Cross, a tall cross with carved figures of the Crucifixion and the Virgin Mary.

Cross at South Harton (Lustleigh, 772822), built into the roadside wall at the farm entrance.

Marchant's Cross (Meavy, 546668) is by the road to Lynch Common, above Marchant's Ford.

Cross at Okehampton (582951). A restored cross, formerly in use as a gatepost, near the west gate of the churchyard.

Cross at Ringhole Copse (South Tawton, 672942), at a road junction a mile to the east of the village has been moved because of roadworks and now overlooks the A30 dual carriageway.

Near Fingle Bridge

Charles' Cross (Moretonhampstead, 743898). A stone pillar with an incised cross, in Charles' Wood, by the track from Fingle Bridge to Cranbrook. (also called Cavalier Cross, see DM No 5.)

Hospit Cross

Challabrook Farm

Sheepstor

Greenaway Cross

Huckworthy Common

Petre's Cross

Wheal Anne Bottom

Leeper Cross

Cheriton Cross

Cross Park

Hospit (Horsepit) Cross (North Bovey, 743847), a cross with a shortened shaft, adapted as a guide stone, at Bovey Cross.

Greenaway Cross previously stood by the lane to Greenaway Farm, Gidleigh, having been re-erected by the DPA. Now in Gidleigh churchyard. (670883)

Cross at Challabrook Farm (Bovey Tracey, 809778), stands by the footpath from the town; at some time used as a gatepost. The inscription on a metal plate dated 1923 claims that the cross had marked the grave of a Royalist officer who fell nearby in 1645.

Cross at Sheepstor (560676), outside the gate of the churchyard. An ancient shaft with modern arms set on a modern base.

Cross at Huckworthy Common (Sampford Spiney, 530711), at a road junction on the edge of the common 400 yards north of Huckworthy Bridge.

Petre's Cross (Forest, 653654). A piece of shaft, inverted, on Western Whittaburrow.

A pillar in Wheal Anne Bottom (Forest, 613695), 800 yards south-east of Nun's Cross Farm, bearing an incised cross, is probably the shaft of a stone cross.

Leeper (Liapa, Leapra) Cross (North Bovey, 702833), on the wall at the entrance to Moorgate.

Cheriton Cross (Cheriton Bishop, 773930), at a road junction in the village, the upper part of a cross on a large socket-stone.

Cross in Cross Park (Lustleigh, 777825) - the head of a cross on a large boulder in a field at Higher Combe.

Swallerton Gate

Swallerton Gate (Manaton, 739791). The head of a cross was recorded by Mr. Masson Phillips in TDA for 1940, lying in the grounds of Hound Tor tea gardens (now a private dwelling). It is now set in the garden wall, facing the road.

Cross at Sticklepath (640940). A very old cross stands on the roof of the Methodist chapel.

Cross at Addiscott (South Tawton, 667933), near the road junction 300 yards to the north of Fire Stone Cross.

Cross at Meavy (540672). An ancient pedestal and shaft with a modern head, under the Meavy Oak.

Moon's Cross (South Tawton, 653941), part of a shaft on a two-stage pedestal, at a road junction 400 yards south of the church.

Cross at Chagford (701875). The war memorial in the churchyard incorporates an ancient cross.

Oxenham Cross (South Tawton, 663944), at the road junction of the same name, 800 yards east of the village.

Cross at Wrangaton (Ugborough, 676578). A large cross by the road that runs through the village.

Cross at Hanger Farm (Cornwood, 612587). An unfinished cross in use as a gatepost by the entrance drive.

Cross at Throwleigh (667907). An ancient socket-stone forms part of the Queen Victoria Jubilee cross in the village.

Shorter Cross (Chagford, 714846). A granite pillar by the road from Week Down to Middlecott, with cruciform devices on two faces.

 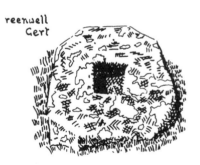

Socket-stones. Left: At Beatland Corner (Shaugh Prior, 548624), a crossroads 800 yards south-east of the village. Right: By the road that skirts the north edge of Wigford Down, near Greenwell Gert, a tinners' gully.

Sticklepath

Addiscott

Meavy

Moon's Cross

Chagford

Oxenham

Wrangaton

Throwleigh

Hanger Farm

Shorter Cross

Sourton Green

Mary
Tavy

South
Zeal

Mary Tavy

Buckland
Court

Bovey
Tracey

church
yard

Shaugh
Prior

Cross in Mary Tavy churchyard (509787), an ancient shaft with a modern head; part of the original head rests on the pedestal.

Fragments on Sourton Green (534903), a socket with the lower part of a shaft; the latter was found in a nearby building in the early 1980s.

Cross at South Zeal (South Tawton, 651935). The village cross, surmounting a three-stage pedestal and socket-stone, stands near the Chapel of SS Mary and Thomas.

Cross at Buckland Court (Buckland in the Moor, 721730), the remains of a rough cross built into the wall on the left of the road when approaching the church from Ausewell Cross.

Cross in Bovey Tracey churchyard (820785), a rebuilt cross which incorporates part of the shaft and one arm of an earlier cross.

Cross at Shaugh Prior (545630). A cross and socket built into the wall near the Vicarage, at the Brag Lane junction east of the church.

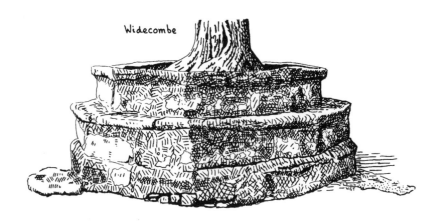

Widecombe

Widecombe (718767). A yew-tree grows from a massive two-stage pedestal near the Church House, assumed to be once the site of the village cross, although there is no sure knowledge. Starkey (1989) recorded what is known of the history of the cross in the churchyard (see page 248). (His account of the relative location of this pedestal and of the other platform nearby is slightly confused.)

Cross on Week Down (Chagford, 712865), a tall cross at the roadside about a mile south-east of the town.

Windy Post (Whitchurch, 534743), north of Feather Tor, on the line of the old route from Chagford to Tavistock.

Watching Place Cross (North Bovey, 713842). A cross at the road junction to the south of Beetor Cross, on the road from Moretonhampstead to Two Bridges.

Cross on Mount Misery (Forest, 637706), at the east corner of Fox Tor Newtake.

Ridding Down (Cornwood, 586612), a cross earlier in use as a gatepost, near Tinpark Farm.

Cross in Widecombe churchyard (718767), a reconstructed cross near the south porch; whether originally the churchyard cross or the village cross is not known - see Starkey 1989.

Cross on Shaden Moor (Shaugh Prior, 552634), an ancient head on a modern shaft, at the roadside between Shaugh village and Cadover Bridge.

Crosses on Ter Hill. (Forest, 641706 and 642706.) Two crosses (one broken and awaiting replacement, 1992), a short distance apart, 1 mile south of Swincombe Farm.

Cross on Walkhampton Common (or **Newleycombe Cross**), on the south side of the old track between Whiteworks and Lowery. 592703.

Whitchurch
Churchyard

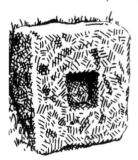

Leigh Lane,
Bickleigh

Socket-stones. Left: Inside the south gate of the churchyard at Whitchurch (493727). Right: At the end of Leigh Lane, Bickleigh, (506625) not far from Roborough.

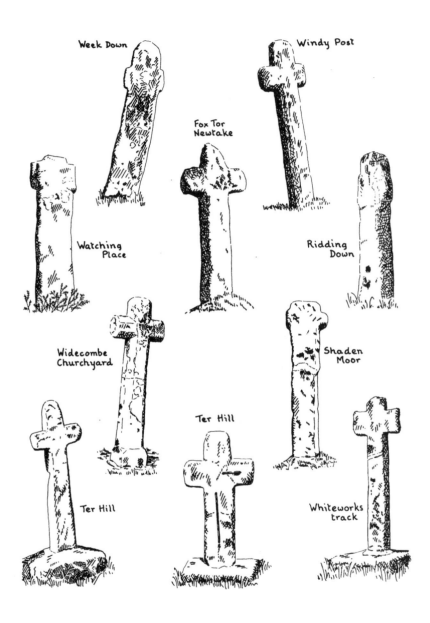

Week Down

Windy Post

Fox Tor
Newtake

Watching
Place

Ridding
Down

Widecombe
Churchyard

Shaden
Moor

Ter Hill

Ter Hill

Whiteworks
track

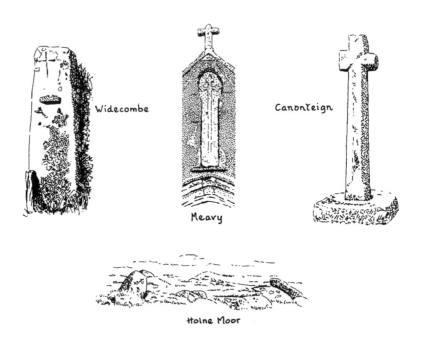

Widecombe

Meavy

Canonteign

Holne Moor

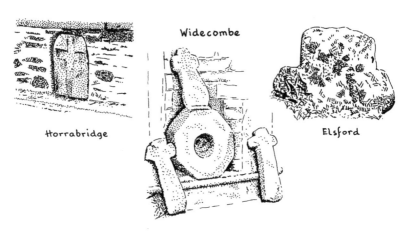

Widecombe

Horrabridge

Elsford

Widecombe (716771). An incised cross on a gatepost at the entrance to the lane leading to Kingshead Farm and Coombe. There is a possibility that it may be associated with the Church Way, which comes down from the moor nearer the village.

Meavy (540672). A slab with a cross in relief - a "coffin lid" or tomb cover - above the window in the south transept gable wall. (There are three other ancient crosses on the church roof.)

Canonteign Barton (Old Canonteign House, Christow, 837832.) The cross is in the garden at the front of the house (photograph in Hoskins' *Devon*, 1954); it was seen by arrangement with the owner, Mr. Edward Gerace.

"Two Thorns Cross" (Holne, 678709). A stone setting which possibly marks the site of a cross on the Buckfast-Tavistock monastic way, about 500 yards west of Venford Reservoir and a similar distance south of the Holne-Hexworthy road - beside two thorn trees. (Discovered in 1982 by Dr. Andrew Fleming, see Hemery 1986a.)

Horrabridge (513699). A stone bearing a cross design, in the parapet of the bridge; possibly a boundary mark.

Widecombe (718768). Three small (finial?) crosses inside the church, discovered when the rood staircase was opened up. They are arranged around an old font which was recovered from the churchyard wall. It is interesting to compare these crosses with the figures and descriptions given by John Chudleigh (1893).

Elsford (Bovey Tracey, 792829). The head of a cross, opposite the lane to Lower Elsford Farm (by the road from Hennock to Moretonhampstead). It was overgrown for a time and rediscovered in the 1980s (Starkey, 1986).

Browney Cross

A socket at Browney Cross, a road junction to the south-west of the Lee Moor china clay area (Shaugh Prior, 544608).

Fragment at Dunsford (813892), a very short piece of shaft with one arm, by the churchyard steps.

Lower Dunstone (Widecombe, 716758). The stumpy cross re-erected here in 1981 was previously in the Vicarage garden.

Fragment at Postbridge (Forest, 651792). In the wall by the gateway of Stannon Lodge is a stone which might possibly be a cross-head with one arm. (Maggie Cross once stood here.)

Socket and shaft at Walkhampton (537702). These pieces lay on the verge opposite Church House after being recovered from a wall nearby, and have since been re-assembled.

Cross in Holne Churchyard (706694), an ancient shaft with new arms on a modern pedestal. (There is also an ancient socket-stone, recut and unrecognisable, incorporated into the war memorial.)

The Bishop's Stone (Lustleigh, 786815). Near the road junction by the old railway station there is a large stone block with a faintly discernible coat-of-arms. It may have been the base of a cross.

Gulwell Cross (Ashburton, 753693). The shaft and arms were recovered from Gulwell Farm and reunited near the Old Totnes Road/West Street junction in 1933 (at Gulwell).

Keble Martin's Chapel

Cross at Keble Martin's Chapel (Buckfastleigh, 666666). An incised cross on a pillar in a small enclosure on the left bank of Wester Wella Brook, 500 yards above its confluence with the Avon. The site is associated with a group of friends who customarily camped in the vicinity between 1904 and 1914; one of them was the Rev. William Keble Martin, author and illustrator of *The Concise British Flora* (1965).

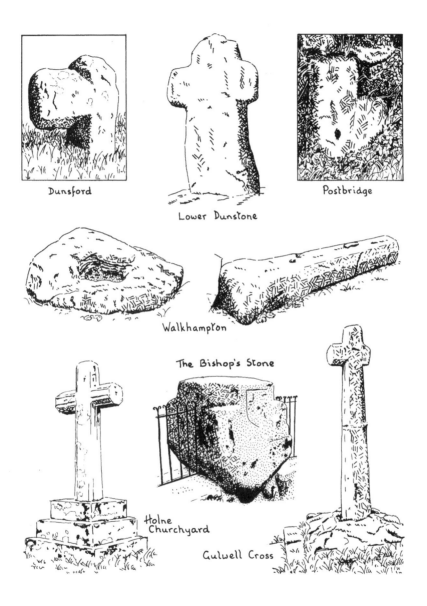

Dunsford

Lower Dunstone

Postbridge

Walkhampton

The Bishop's Stone

Holne
Churchyard

Gulwell Cross

Hameldon Cross (Widecombe/ Manaton, 704801), a one-armed cross SSE of Hameldon Tor, which has been used as a boundary stone. (Inscribed HC DS 1854.)

Hameldon Cross

Some modern crosses

Widgery Cross (Lydford, 539856), on Bra (Brat, Brai) Tor, otherwise Widgery Tor, was erected by the artist of that name to commemorate Queen Victoria's Golden Jubilee.

Sherril (Sherwell) Cross (Widecombe, 683738), on Corn Down, above the road from Ouldsbroom to Babeny, is a memorial to a member of the Cave-Penney family who lived at Sherril.

Cross at Hexworthy (Forest, 656726), a Queen Victoria Jubilee cross near the Forest Inn.

Drivage Bottom (Walkhampton, 599699). A memorial cross inscribed "SLH 1887-1966", in an ancient socket-stone, by the Devonport Leat ½ mile west of Nun's Cross, on the route of the Abbot's Way; commemorates Mrs.S.L.Hutchinson. Drivage Bottom derives its name from a mining term, and refers to the small valley into which the Devonport Leat tunnel opens.

Cross at Urgles (Meavy, 535649). A modern cross and socket-stone opposite the entrance to Urgles Farm, Goodameavy. The ancient socket-stone from this site is at Goodameavy House.

Cross at Dunnabridge Farm (Forest, 639738), a memorial cross of the early 20th century, standing by the West Dart on private land opposite Little Sherberton.

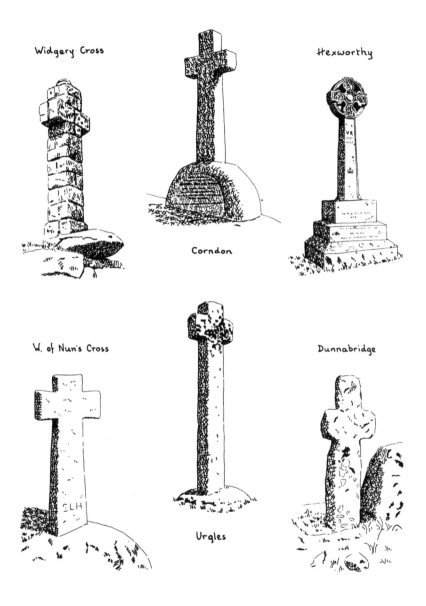

Widgery Cross

Corndon

Hexworthy

W. of Nun's Cross

Urgles

Dunnabridge

Apart from those I have included elsewhere (e.g. the cross at Sourton Down) there are, or have been, other crosses and numerous fragments, possibles, doubtfuls, crosses recorded but not traceable, and so on. I am listing a few of them below.

Bovey Tracey (817785). The town or market cross; an ancient shaft (a pointed pillar) with a new head, incorporated into the war memorial.

Buckland in the Moor (720731). A tree grows from a massive two-stage pedestal outside the south gate of the churchyard.

Coombe Tor (Chagford, 686871). A modern cross in enclosures overlooking East and West Coombe.

Dunsford (828894). At Six-mile Hill Cross, or Two Crosses. An old cross stands in a hedge overlooking the crossroads a mile to the east of the village.

Fox Tor Newtake. In addition to the massive cross at Mount Misery there was the broken head of another cross lying nearby; this disappeared many years ago.

Haredon (Ugborough, 675552). A shaft with one arm missing and the other damaged, in use as a gatepost in the farmyard. Previously at Dunwell, nearby.

Holystreet (Chagford, 688877). The cross which was once in the wall here (and previously apparently in the town) now forms part of the war memorial in the churchyard.

Hookmoor Cross (Ugborough, 685568). The stump of a cross (its head disappeared in the 1930s) in use as a guide-stone.

Lowery (Walkhampton, 556693). Nothing relevant can now be seen at the site of a cross on the "Monks' Path" from Buckfast, which comes down over Walkhampton Common. The cross is thought to have stood opposite the gate of the farm.

Three Barrows (Ugborough, 651626?). The broken head of a cross with one arm missing is said to lie among the clitter approx. north-west of the north-west barrow.

Throwleigh (669908). Part of a cross-shaft was found in the wall of the Barton in 1977 (TDA 116, 1984), and has been set up in the churchyard.

___Commemorative Marks___

The earliest commemorative marks to be seen on Dartmoor are doubtless the prehistoric barrows (not necessarily the stone cairns), which it is reasonable to assume were established to mark the burial sites of respected members of the community. It has been suggested that menhirs were early tombstones, to be succeeded by inscribed Celtic memorial stones, and ultimately by the modern headstone (Baring-Gould, 1907).

Among the well-known commemorative marks there are rocks with inscriptions, including the "Ten Commandments stones" on Buckland Beacon, a massive boulder in Wistman's Wood recording details of a tree felled there in 1866, the Hunters' Stone near Shipley Bridge, and some rocks in the Cowsic at Beardown; and there are tablets attached to rocks and pillars, such as the Crossing memorial at Duck's Pool and the Phillpotts peat pass markers.

The story of the William Donaghy memorial by the East Dart under Hartland Tor is given by Brian Sugg in DM No 5, 1986.

I mention but one of a number of new commemorative marks - a small metal cross ($3\frac{3}{4}$" high x $1\frac{1}{2}$" across the arms) affixed to a boulder on Hand Hill (Forest, 612693) in 1980; its story is detailed briefly in DM No 5.

Tablet at Hennock

The Hunters' Stone

A memorial tablet at the gateway to Hennock churchyard (830809). The date is 1603.

The Hunters' Stone (South Brent, 681632) near the Avon above Shipley Bridge, commemorates personalities well-known in local hunting circles. It was described by Crossing in *One Hundred Years* (1901), and among the several inscriptions there are two of recent date.

The Coffin Stone (Widecombe, 677733), by the old track on Dartmeet Hill, bears initials (of which probably two sets are recent vandalism) and incised crosses. The stone was conveniently sited for placing a coffin whilst its bearers took a rest during the climb up the hill. Folklore relates the devastating effect of a thunderbolt which consumed the remains of an unsavoury individual and split the rock

A memorial stone on Hameldon (Manaton, 714806) bears the initials of the crew of a Hampden bomber, which crashed here during the Second World War.

Stephen's Grave (Peter Tavy, 536781). The stone, re-erected by the DPA in 1936, commemorates a suicide, John Stephens of Peter Tavy, a youthful victim of the infidelity of his betrothed.

A headstone in Lydford churchyard, representative of several of similar pattern in the area, with a very emotive inverted heart design.

A peat pass marker (Forest, 620825) about 80 yards WSW of Stat's House on Marsh Hill. A review of the Phillpotts peat passes of northern Dartmoor, carried out by Brian le Messurier (TDA 1965) recorded nearly a dozen of them, most being marked with memorial plaques. The wording is: "This stone marks a crossing through the peat, which may be of use to hunting and cattlemen; the crossing was made by Frank Phillpotts, who died October 1909, it is kept up in his memory by his brother and son".

Jay's Grave (Manaton, 732799), said to be the grave of a local girl, Kitty Jay, who had been seduced and committed suicide, is to be found where the path from Natsworthy Gate emerges on to Swine Down.

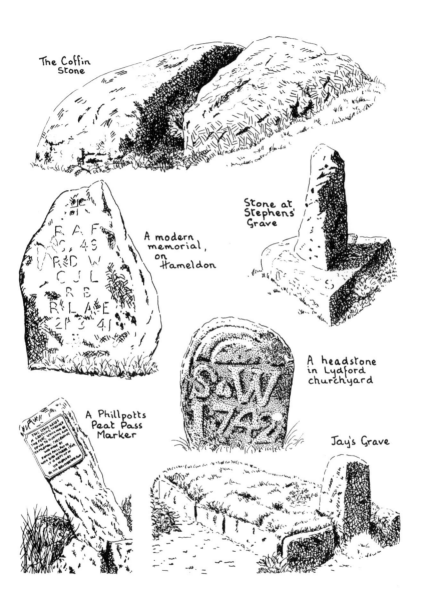

The Coffin Stone

A modern memorial, on Hameldon

R.A.F.
G. 49
R & D W
C J L
R B
R' L A E
21 3 41

Stone at Stephens' Grave

A headstone in Lydford churchyard

S D W
1 7 4 2

A Phillpotts Peat Pass Marker

Jay's Grave

_____ Boundary Marks _____

Dartmoor is far from being an exception to the universal practice of defining the limits of administrative areas. The two classes of boundary which immediately come to mind as relevant to this region are those of the Forest and the parishes. Parish boundaries were established in the twelfth century, when the manor system was at its height.

Sometimes the boundaries follow streams, or are marked by other natural features like rock piles or individual rocks. In some cases use has been made of objects raised by prehistoric man, such as menhirs and cairns. Other man-made marks, though more recent than these, may even so be of considerable age or importance; they include those associated with tinning and other industries. The subject also includes relatively modern marks; among them are items relating to railways, water undertakings and recent industry, and a wide range of miscellaneous marks.

(See Dave Brewer's *Field Guide to the Boundary Markers on and Around Dartmoor*, 1986.)

---------------- ✦ ----------------

Boundary stones on Hameldon. Among the marks set up by the Duke of Somerset to emphasise the limits of Natsworthy Manor are several stones dated 1854 on the ridge of Hameldon. The marks towards the north of the ridge follow the Widecombe/Manaton boundary line. Between Hameldon Cross and the head of the East Webburn are **Gray Weather** (707803) and **Blue Jug** (708803). South of Hameldon Cross a number of prehistoric barrows are marked - **Broad Barrow** (705799), **Single Barrow** (706795), **Two Barrows** (706792), **Hameldon Beacon** (708789), and, changing direction south-eastward, **Old House** (714786). Between the last two barrows there is a natural boulder confusingly called the Grey Wethers Stone. (See "Pit" and "Slade's Well".) The bounds of the manors within the parish of Widecombe have been well researched, and are included in Dave Brewer's *Guide*.

Grey Wethers

Single Barrow

Two Barrows

Broad Barrow

Blue Jug

Hameldon Beacon

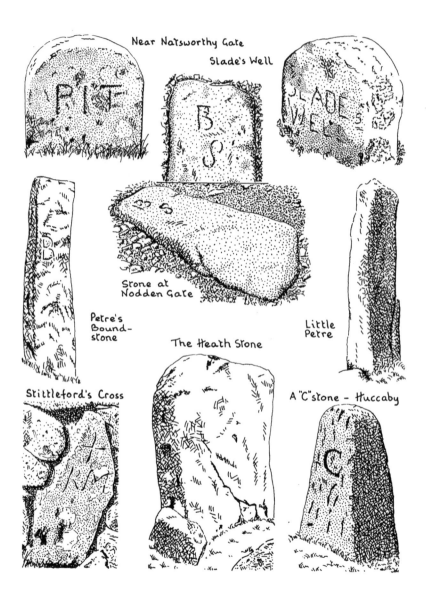

Near Natsworthy Gate

Slade's Well

Stone at
Nodden Gate

Petre's
Bound-
stone

Little
Petre

The Heath Stone

Stittleford's Cross

A "C" stone - Huccaby

More "DS stones" on the Natsworthy Manor boundary. **"Pit"** (721802), referring to a small quarry, is at the roadside at Natsworthy Gate, where the north boundary comes down the East Webburn from Blue Jug. The southern boundary crosses the Widecombe valley from Hameldon and mounts the Chinkwell/Honeybag ridge, here marked by **Slade's Well** (728784).

A **"Bridestowe and Sourton stone"** (two views) in use as a sill at Nodden Gate (530863). It has since been re-erected.

Petre's Bound Stone (659690) stands on Ryder's Hill; here a prehistoric cairn marks the point where the parishes of Holne and Buckfastleigh adjoin the Forest. The "B" refers to the Buckfastleigh boundary. There was another stone here called Petre on the Mount - a Holne stone with an incised "H"; this disappeared (see DM Winter 1986) and another stone was subsequently put up in its place. There are numerous other markers on parish boundaries in this area, including some at named points e.g. Filfer Head, Bourne's Pit and Rounder's Hole.

Little Petre (654655) is a plain pillar on the Forest/South Brent boundary about 130 yards NNE of Petre's Cross.

Stittleford's Cross (Stentiford's Cross on the 6 inch map), at an angle in the wall a few yards south-east of White Gate (742761), is inscribed with a cross and the initials "RM" (Rawlin Mallock, a Lord of the Manor of Dunstone). It terminates a row of stones which comes up from the Grey Goose Nest (740757) at the edge of Blackslade Mire, here marking the boundary between Ilsington and Widecombe.

The Heath Stone (671837), though standing within Chagford parish, is an ancient forest bond-mark, just south of the road from Tawton Gate to Fernworthy before it enters the plantation. Since 1970 the stone has borne a biblical inscription (see Hemery, 1983a).

A **"C stone"** near Huccaby Bridge (659729). The maintenance of a highway crossing a bridge was once the responsibility of the county before highways in general became their concern. "C stones", of which there are quite a number on Dartmoor, marked the limits of that responsibility on either side of the bridge.

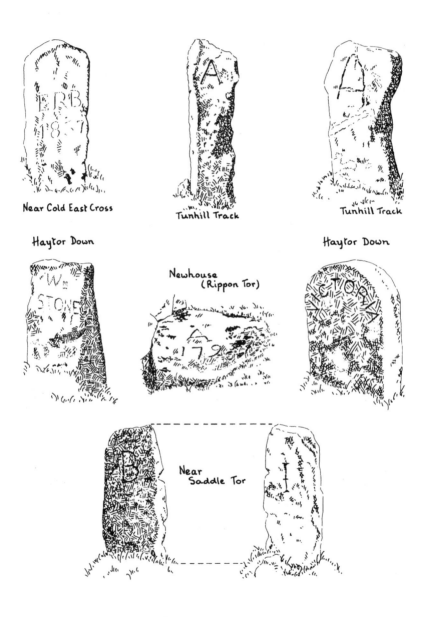

Near Cold East Cross

Tunhill Track

Tunhill Track

Haytor Down

Newhouse
(Rippon Tor)

Haytor Down

Near
Saddle Tor

Top row: **Stones near Cold East Cross.** There is a series of manorial/parish boundary markers running southwards from Blackslade Ford (736752), west of the Ashburton/Manaton road (see map in Brewer, 1986). Some of them are inscribed "EPB 1837" (Edmund Pollexfen Bastard, then Lord of the Manor of Buckland in the Moor). One is a "PW" stone (see page 267) and all are on the Ashburton/Buckland boundary. The two rough pillars I have illustrated (738748 and 738749) bear only the initial letters of these parishes.

Middle row, left and right: **Haytor Down.** A series of stones begins near the 6-mile stone of the Haytor Granite Tramway (780774) and runs WNW towards Houndtor Combe. Several of them bear the initials "DS" and the date 1853, the Duke of Somerset bounds here coinciding with the parish boundaries of Ilsington/Manaton and Ilsington/Bovey Tracey. **Old William** and **Victoria** are at 771779 and 766782. Others in the series are Prince Albert, Owlacombe Burrow, Old Jack, the Prince of Wales and the Hole Stone. A three-sided pillar marks the point where the three parishes meet.

Centre: **An Ashburton boundary marker.** An earthbound boulder inscribed "A 1793", on the boundary with Ilsington, at the roadside opposite Newhouse. 741756.

Bottom: **Stone near Saddle Tor** (754756). This pillar, near the road to the north-east of the tor, is one of the marks associated with the manor of Bagtor. The main run of marks is on a line between the Duke Stone (was missing - replacement stone erected 11th May 1993, in memory of Harry Starkey; 754765, by Becka brook opposite Holwell Farm) and Crownley Parks. One of these, a short distance below the road, consists of the same letters "B" and "I" (referring to Bagtor in the parish of Ilsington) incised on the upper surface of a large boulder at one of the sites known as "The Blacksmiths' Shop" (757764), illustrated on page 269. On the western boundary of the manor (adjoining Widecombe Town Manor) there is a similarly incised stone in the wall that runs NNW from White Gate (120 yards beyond Seven Lords Lands barrow - itself an important bond-mark), and beyond this, a recently re-erected pillar at Hawkeswell.

Trendlebere Down (779792). A rough pillar standing at the roadside (Lower Terrace Drive), on the Bovey/Lustleigh boundary, inscribed with a "Y" for Yarner. There is a Lustleigh/Manaton stone by the same road (opposite side) a mile nearer Manaton (768797).

A **"DCP stone"** at the junction of the Omen Beam road with the Tavistock-Two Bridges highway (Forest, 595749) is one of several markers relating to the prison enclosures. Dave Brewer (1986) explains that the inscription refers to an earlier name for the prison authority, the "Directors of Convict Prisons".

A **parish boundary stone,** opposite The Woodpecker (once the Carew Arms), where the Ugborough/South Brent boundary, following Glaze Brook, crosses the A38 trunk road. 694589.

A **"PW stone"** on the Ilsington/Buckland boundary (739745) 300 yards NNW of Cold East Cross. There is another, similarly inscribed, between Cold East Cross and Rushlade Bridge (743738). They refer to Philip Woodley, Lord of the Manor of Halshanger.

Willsworthy stones. For most of its course the boundary of the Willsworthy firing range follows that of Willsworthy Manor. Here, at 526818, near the Mine Leat north-east of Wheal Jewell reservoir, one of the range markers stands alongside a manor boundary stone. In this case the B of the Willsworthy Bounds initials (on the opposite face) could be mistaken for a D. (See map in Brewer 1986.)

A **warren boundary post** on the north-east slope of Cosdon (640924) inscribed "DC2/SZ2", referring to an agreement between the Duchy of Cornwall and the commoners of South Zeal. There is another post, at 633933 (Stumpy Post) inscribed "DC1/SZ1".

Cow Bridge (661864), a large rock raised up on smaller stones (not a bridge) on the Chagford/Gidleigh boundary, near the enclosure wall between the entrance to Batworthy and Batworthy Corner. The letter inscribed on it is said to be a G.

Trendlebere Down

Carew Arms

Ughborough

Princetown

Willsworthy

Near Dry Bridge

Skaigh Warren

Cow Bridge

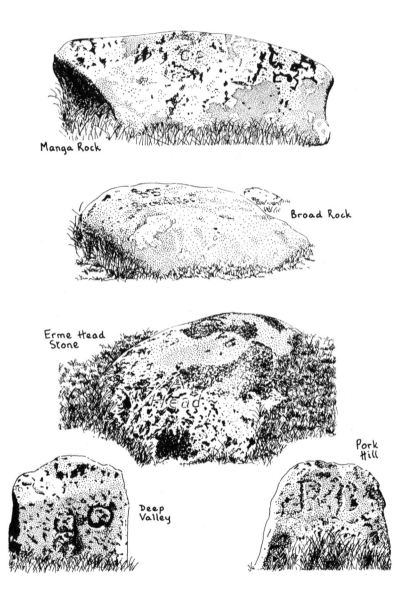

Manga Rock

Broad Rock

Erme Head Stone

Deep Valley

Pork Hill

Manga Rock (Forest/Gidleigh, 636858), a large boulder on a spur between the North Teign and its tributary Wood (Hew, OS Hugh) Lake, inscribed "GP" (Gidleigh parish).

Broad Rock (Forest/Cornwood/Sheepstor, 618672), a low boulder in an area of scattered rocks, 400 yards north-west of Erme Head, is a Forest bond-mark, and also serves for Blachford Manor, Cornwood. Inscribed "BB" (Blachford Bounds) and "Broad Rock".

Erme Head Stone (Forest/Cornwood, 620673), 200 yards ENE of Broad Rock, is another low boulder and also perhaps not easily located at the first attempt. The inscription "A Head" (i.e. Arme Head) is very faint.

The stone at the head of Deep Valley (544895), i.e. above Withycombe Bottom, is on the line dividing Sourton parish from the lands common to Bridestowe and Sourton, and 300 yards or so to the SSE of Sourton Tors. On one side is an incised "B", and on the other a device which looks like 9°.

An "RB" stone (525754). There is a row of stones inscribed "RB", east of the road to Higher Godsworthy, and about 150 yards from the Tavistock-Two Bridges road. Whilst they are on the Whitchurch/Peter Tavy boundary, they have obviously served another purpose - Dave Brewer discusses a possible connection with a one-time local family called Reep.

The Blacksmiths' Shop (757764). See page 265.

Harford/Ugborough boundary stones. The stones of the prehistoric row between Butterdon Hill and Piles Hill were utilised to form a section of this very long line of boundary markers. Some of the later stones are inscribed with the initial letters of the relevant parishes. Those illustrated, near Sharp Tor (Higher Piles, 651618) and near the head of Left Lake (646635) (Crossing calls this the "U stone") are near the track of the old Red Lake Railway. The stone by Red Lake (the "Outer U stone", 643664) marks the point where the two parishes adjoin the Forest.

The Longstone, (655582) between Butterdon Hill and Western Beacon, on the same line, is not a prehistoric menhir as some other "Longstones" are.

A "CB" stone. This marker, at the roadside on the edge of Soussons Down plantation, is one of four so inscribed, referring to Cator bounds. There is one by the Church Path a short distance westwards, and two others on the line of a reave which here marks the Manaton/ Widecombe boundary, and runs towards the Wallabrook between Runnage Bridge and Pizwell. 677786.

Headland Warren boundary stones. There is a series of markers, generally inscribed "WB", delineating the boundary of Headland Warren. Crossing speculated as to whether the "WB" on Benet's Cross stands for William Benet, a tinners' juror in the time of Henry VIII, or whether it, along with the "WBs" on the other stones, represents "Warren Bounds". It is interesting to note that one of the series, at the roadside on Shapley Common (695816) spells out "Warren Bounds" in full. The other stone illustrated (696808) is one of three near the foot of the track that leads up to Grimspound. Dave Brewer discusses variations of the "WB" inscriptions.

Red Lake

Piles Hill

Left Lake

The Long Stone   Butterdon Hill

Ephraim's
Pinch

Shapley Common

Firth
Bridge

Dick's Well

Staple Tor / Roos Tor

Roos Tor

Shaugh Moor / Lee Moor

Huntingdon Mine track

Hole Rock

SM 1835

LM

The stone near Dick's Well (551861) stands at the boundary between the lands common to Bridestowe and Sourton and the Forest, and is inscribed "BS", and "L" for Lydford.

North of Great Staple Tor is a stone on the Peter Tavy/Whitchurch boundary. 543763.

Roos Tor (Peter Tavy, 543766) is encircled by a series of fourteen pillars each with an incised "B". Near at least twelve of them, cut into the surface of a natural rock, is a device consisting of a circle about 10 inches in diameter with a central bisecting line. These marks were set up in about 1880, in an area of intensive granite working, to indicate the protective limits imposed by the then Duke of Bedford on the taking of stone. Similar marks had been set up around Pew Tor to define the limits of 1847. There are nine of them, similar to the Roos Tor marks but each consisting of a circle divided by a cross. The protective area was extended in 1896, and each of the four corners marked with a variation of this symbol - a smaller circle-and-cross with the addition of five holes, one at each intersection on the design. When Dave Brewer wrote in 1986 the whereabouts of only three of these marks was known. See Helen Harris, TDA 113, 1981.

Shaugh Moor/Lee Moor (Shaugh Prior). The stone at the roadside (567636) a mile south-east of Cadover Bridge is dated about the time the china clay industry began in that area. Emmet's Post, on a cairn nearby (568632) is one of those similarly inscribed. South-west of Shell Top there are others bearing the initials "LM" and "PM" (Lee Moor/ Penn Moor).

Near the Huntingdon Mine track from Lud Gate, a rough pillar on the Buckfastleigh/Dean Prior boundary (676670).

Hole Rock (Ilsington/Manaton, 756785). In Houndtor Combe there is a circular stone with a central depression, one of the series of marks on the Ilsington boundary on Haytor Down. The pillar beside it, the "Hole Stone", is inscribed "HS".

South Hessary Tor

Left: **Barn Hill** (Whitchurch, 536745). A pillar inscribed "SB" stands about 20 paces below the Grimstone and Sortridge Leat, 300 yards south of the site of the Blacksmiths' Shop, and opposite a point about half-way along the nearly-detached part of Sampford Spiney parish (the "Ace of Diamonds"). These initials occur elsewhere in this locality - there is an inscribed boulder at 540748 (indicated on the 6 inchmap), and another at 541744, 85 paces NW of an "SB/WB" pillar which marks the eastern point of the diamond.

Right: **An "SSP" stone,** marking the southern point of the Sampford Spiney diamond, 300 yards SW of Vixen Tor. ("WB" on the opposite face.) 540739.

Centre: **South Hessary Tor,** 597723. One of the Forest bond-marks on the Walkhampton boundary, a small and very rusted metal post affixed to a rock at the summit of the tor.

Stones on Riddon Ridge. In tin-streaming days there was no doubt a jealous guarding of claims, and there is a 16th century record, mentioned by Mary and Jessica Walmesley (1982), which describes how a tinner would cut turves to make his corner bounds. Hemery (1983a) drew attention to a stone on the right bank of the Wallabrook below Pizwell Bridge, inscribed with the letters "FS" and an "H" below, and others on Riddon Ridge and at Middle Cator, which he thought could be tinners' bounds. The stones illustrated are (top to bottom) at 665766 (near a large hut-circle), 666765, and 667763. There is another stone, at 668762, inscribed "RHR" on one side and "TS/H" on the other. Just above Snaily House there is a marker inscribed "SL" (661762).

Riddon Ridge

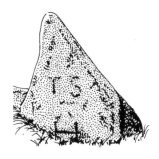

Guide Stones

Mention has been made of the Phillpotts peat passes of northern Dartmoor, some of which are marked by pillars bearing memorial tablets, and if we go back several centuries we can connect many of the old stone crosses with routes across the moor. The erection of crosses for this purpose was later discontinued, and simple stones or pillars were used, usually with inscriptions indicating the directions to the relevant border towns. Apart from the significance of these inscriptions, usually consisting only of initial letters, there is little or nothing to distinguish many of the markers from boundary stones.

Chagford Cross (North Bovey, 688828). A roughly cubic block at the road junction a mile north-east of Benet's Cross, giving directions to Tavistock, Chagford and Moreton. (The junction is sometimes called Shapley Cross; there are other Chagford Crosses, eg. at Murchington and at Moretonhampstead.)

Stoney Post Cross (Gallantry Bower, Holne, 717702). At the road junction south of Chasegate, a pillar with raised initial letters denoting Ashburton, Buckfastleigh and Tavistock.

White (Hemsworthy) Gate. A pillar at the roadside (Widecombe, 741762) near the Ilsington boundary. In transverse section the pillar is a truncated wedge, each of the wider faces bearing an initial - "A" for Ashburton, "B" for Bovey, and "M" for Moreton or possibly Manaton.

Beetor Cross (North Bovey, 713843). At the road junction a short distance north of the Watching Place, and nearly three miles from Moretonhampstead, a pillar with the incised initials of Moreton, Chagford and Tavistock.

Week Cross (North Bovey, 727851). At the crossroads a mile nearer Moretonhampstead, near the entrance to the Manor House Hotel, a stone with initials indicating Newton, Moreton, Chagford and Tavistock.

Woodman's Corner (Walkhampton/Buckland Monachorum, 527684). At a road junction $\frac{1}{2}$ mile north-east of Yelverton on the Moreton road, a stone with the self-explanatory abbreviations "Ply", "Moor" and "Walkht".

Long Ash Hill. See page 279.

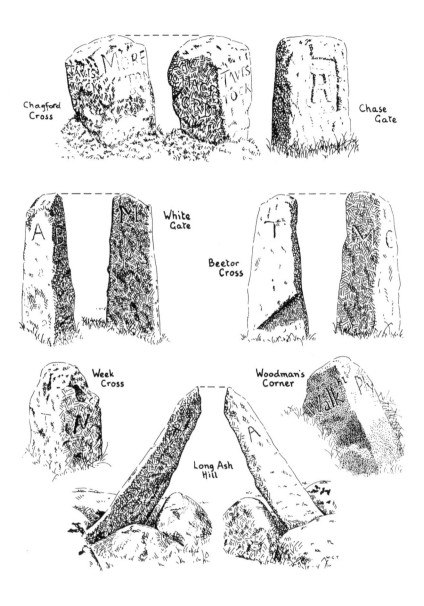

Chagford
Cross

Chase
Gate

White
Gate

Beetor
Cross

Week
Cross

Woodman's
Corner

Long Ash
Hill

Long Ash Hill

Near Yellow-meade

Long Ash Hill

Swin-combe Farm

Moor Cross - Dean Prior

Greenawell - previously at Bughead Cross

Stone Cross

Cross Furzes

"T-A stones". At a roadside gateway on the hill east of Merrivale Bridge is a post inscribed with the letters "T" and "A". This was taken from a series of pillars which marked the course of the old Tavistock-Ashburton track. The principal surviving section begins at a post on the edge of the common (Walkhampton, 552750) just above "Hillside", and runs over Long Ash Hill to a point 750 yards south of North Hessary Tor. There is then a long gap before reaching the penultimate stone on the far side of Royal Hill, and 550 yards further east, the post at Swincombe Farm (Forest, 639726).

Moor Cross (Dean Prior, 704639). A stone with the incised initials of Ashburton, Tavistock, Totnes and Plymouth.

Greenawell (North Bovey, 730860). A stone with the initial letters of Okehampton, Moreton and Newton (the "N" is reversed), in the farmyard; previously at Bughead Cross (North Bovey/Moretonhampstead, 734854), a short distance to the SSE.

Stone Cross (Buckland in the Moor, 719745). At the road junction a mile north of Buckland Church, a stone with inscriptions "Ashburton", " 1790 Newton" and "W" (for Widecombe) .

Cross Furzes (Buckfastleigh, 699668). At the junction of the Lud Gate lane and the Scorriton road, a stone with the raised letters "A", "T" and "B" (Ashburton, Tavistock and Buckfastleigh - possibly Brent but less likely).

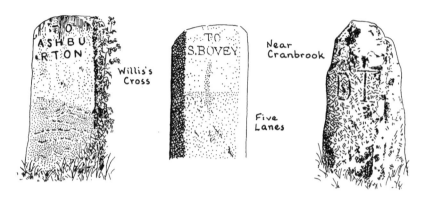

Willis's Cross (Ilsington, 799753). A pillar of truncated wedge-shaped section, indicating directions to Ashburton, Newton and Ilsington. Posts with inscriptions in a similar style are common on the eastern side of the moor.

Five Lanes. 830801. A five-sided guide-post on the Hennock/Bovey Tracey boundary, indicating directions to Chudleigh, Exeter, Hennock, Moreton and S. Bovey (i.e. South Bovey, otherwise Bovey Tracey).

Near Cranbrook Castle (Moretonhampstead, 742888). A rough pillar with initials DT, C, M and E (Drewsteignton, Chagford, Moreton and Exeter) standing at the end of the lane which goes towards Cranbrook Castle and Fingle Bridge.

———————————— ✦ ————————————

In 1991 I drew attention to an inscribed post, which I had discovered several years earlier (whilst researching gateposts). It stands at an infilled gateway in the wall of Bellever Plantation a short distance SW of Postbridge. The significance of this post, with P and M on opposite faces, no doubt referring to Plymouth and Moretonhampstead, has been discussed by Dave Brewer (in DM Autumn 1991), who mentions one other similarly inscribed (now in use as a door-jamb in a barn at Lettaford).

Milestones

Whilst there are some later and more conventional milestones on Dartmoor, there are others, sometimes in out-of-the-way places, which deserve more than a passing glance, owing to their age, design, location or purpose.

Lydford

Lydford. An old milestone near the church, indicating distances from Tavistock and Okehampton. Among other stones of this type is one recorded by Dave Brewer (DAS Newsletter No 36, Jan 1987) indicating 1 mile from Tavistock and 16 miles from Okehampton, and also giving the date 1755 (at Hurdwick, 473758).

Rundlestone Corner (Forest, 576749). An example of the standard design of milestones to be seen beside the main roads across the moor. These were set up probably in connection with the Turnpike Trusts in the early 1800s - see Dave Brewer in DM Winter 1990.

Exeter Lane (Tavistock/Mary Tavy, 493754). There is a series of milestones along the Tavistock-Okehampton highway; they are obviously very old and are shaped like headstones. Those towards the north give only distances "From Oakhampton", whilst towards the south the distances are given "From Tavistock", "Oakhampton" and "Truro". A later stone, in Tavistock, gives distances from London, Okehampton, Callington and Truro. Halfway between Tavistock and Okehampton there is a metal pillar giving the distance as 8 miles from (or hopefully "to") each of these towns.

Rundlestone Corner

Exeter Lane

Near Lustleigh

One "miol" from Widecombe

Haytor Granite Tramway

Pennycomequick (Whitchurch Down)

Zeal Tor Tramway

Green Lane (Whitchurch Down)

Lustleigh (786823). Between Newton Abbot and Moretonhampstead there are milestones which give distances in miles, furlongs and chains. The stone illustrated was broken off in the mid-1980s and repaired.

Widecombe (722780). A stone in the roadside wall nearly opposite Stouts Cottages on the Natsworthy road is probably associated with the limits allowed to prisoners-of-war billeted out from Princetown in the early 19th century, but not proven. There are other "1 mile stones" with more substantial claims to this purpose, related to well-known "parole towns". (Brewer, 1986.)

Haytor Down. The milestones associated with the Haytor granite tramway refer to the distances from the terminus at Ventiford. The 6-mile stone stands near the Widecombe-Bovey road a short distance below the Green Lane turn-off (Bovey Tracey/Ilsington 780773); 15 paces behind it, in a furze bush, stands the John Stone, the first in the line of boundary stones across Haytor Down. No 5 is in Yarner Wood (Bovey Tracey, 785784), and No 4 is 20 yards from Chapple Road (Lower Down, Bovey Tracey, 799781) within private woodland (Colehayes Plantation). No 3 is behind a row of cottages near the Pottery Pond in Bovey Tracey (811772), and Nos 1 and 2 cannot be found.

Milestones on Whitchurch Down. The pillar south-west of **Pennycomequick** (514739) at the roadside between Moorshop and Warren's Cross bears a diagonal inscription "13 miles to Plym°". The stone beyond the opposite end of the golf course (**Green Lane,** 492740) is inscribed "14 miles to Plym°" and "1T" (1 mile to Tavistock).

Zeal Tor Tramroad. Near the branch that goes to Petre's Pits there are a couple of quarter mile stones. Crossing mentioned two stones in this area (Broad Rushes) which indicate the distance to Shipley Bridge, one being marked " $\frac{1}{4}$ ". I wonder whether he meant $\frac{3}{4}$ because I also found two stones, one (collapsed in a gully) on which I could discern "2 mile" (without an "s"), and another, $1\frac{3}{4}$ miles from Shipley Bridge, marked " $\frac{3}{4}$ " (664646). Hemery refers to the stones as $\frac{1}{2}$ mile and $\frac{3}{4}$ mile, and states that the distances are from Crossways.

Part IX
MISCELLANEA

The old toll-house at South Brent (697601) is one of a row of properties in Church Street. Attached to its wall is a board listing a scale of market tolls. (It has no connection with the turnpike trusts.)

The Prison

Princetown was founded at about the end of the 18th century by Sir Thomas Tyrwhitt, Dartmoor's renowned industrial pioneer, a Member of Parliament, and Lord Warden of the Stannaries. Among his proposed schemes were the cultivation of this area of central Dartmoor, the development of granite working, on that part of Walkhampton Common to the west of the settlement, the construction of the Plymouth and Dartmoor Railway to transport the products of his undertakings, and the promotion of the Princetown to Tavistock highway.

As part of his plan to open up this part of the moor, Tyrwhitt proposed that a prison should be built to accommodate French prisoners-of-war, many of whom were incarcerated in overcrowded hulks in Plymouth Sound. Building began in 1806 and the first prisoners arrived in 1809. Four years later the French were joined by Americans, and the establishment continued as a war prison until the beginning of 1816. After that time the buildings remained empty (apart from a short period as a naphtha works) until 1850 when their use as a convict prison began.

Although the gaol is to many of those unacquainted with the region the only significance attached to the word "Dartmoor", the area it covers is relatively minute in the context of the moor as a whole. To the enthusiast it is big enough, however, and his or her concern is likely to be related to the access limitations imposed by the attached acreage, largely the prison farm. The question of the future use of the site periodically comes up for discussion, and should the present restrictions ever be removed there will certainly be a number of features the enthusiast will be anxious to investigate.

____The Military Presence ____

It is an unfortunate fact that Dartmoor's status as a National Park has been demonstrated as taking second place to other roles . One of the most difficult of those aspects which the conservationist argues against is the use of the moor for military training. The recorded history of such use goes back several centuries, and at present the whole of Dartmoor is a military training ground, where the unquestionable importance of preparedness must be equated with frequent loss to the public of many thousands of acres, while live firing takes place.

The obtrusive indications of the current military occupation of Dartmoor tend to increase in a quite relentless manner, and are naturally deprecated by the enthusiast; however, there are several signs of earlier activity which may well demand the explorer's attention. And so another field of study, military archaeology, is taking shape, exemplifying the "Dartmoor enthusiast's paradox" I mentioned in my preface.

The old rifle ranges of the mid-19th century immediately come to mind. There are eight granite butts above the head of Butter Brook (in the central southern section of square 6560). During a chance meeting in that area between the author and Mr.C.E. (Ted) Birkett Dixon in 1974, two 100-yard markers were found. Ted subsequently led an expedition which discovered a series extending to 800 yards (i.e. beyond the Ugborough boundary east of its intersection with the track of the old Red Lake Railway).

The future of the more recently abandoned Rippon Tor rifle range (Ashburton, 7573) came under discussion some years ago, and it seems that it is likely to be preserved, in a reversal of a system which has demanded or condoned the destruction of too many legacies of Dartmoor's modern history.

Range
marker
- Hart
Tor

Range marker, Hart Tor. On the disused range (5872) between Hart
Tor and the site of the old Devil's Bridge south-west of Princetown the
distances are marked by granite pillars.

(illustrated overleaf)
Range markers, Harford Moor (653600 and 655608). The range here
was established in 1861.

Observation Post No 15 on Okement Hill (one of a number of such
features in this locality), and the **hut on Steeperton Tor** are representative of a diversity of incongruous features associated with military
activity.

Range boundaries are marked by red-and-white posts, and warning
notices are placed at various relevant points. The three ranges
(Okehampton, Merrivale and Willsworthy) cover the greater part of
the open moor west of a line from South Zeal to Two Bridges.

Danger signals are displayed from prominent sites near the range
boundaries when firing is in progress (red flags by day and red lights
at night).

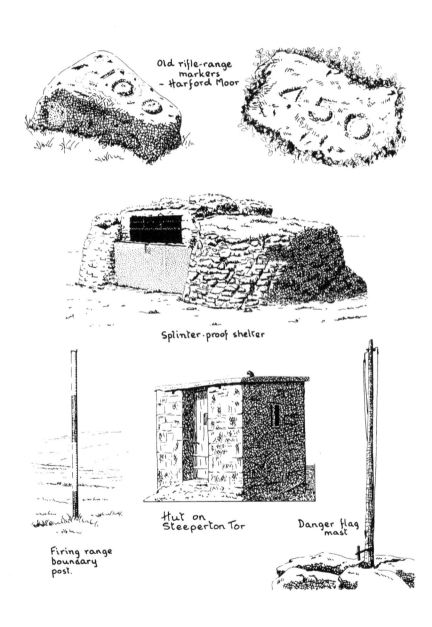

Old rifle-range markers – Harford Moor

Splinter-proof shelter

Firing range boundary post.

Hut on Steeperton Tor

Danger flag mast

Follies

The history and nature of follies are complex. In general, however, they are sham structures, built under the dictates of fashion, some designed to look like the ruins of older fabrications, serving little or no useful purpose, apart from adding interest to the scene, or providing shelter from which a view could be obtained over the surrounding country-side, or merely boosting the ego of their owners.

There are few features within the National Park to which the term "folly" can be attached, and Princep's Folly, on Gidleigh Tor (671878), is the only one which uses the term as a part of its name. However, this structure, now represented merely by vestigial remains, was not intended to be a folly in the generally accepted meaning of the word. It was a house built, in 1846, in a very unpractical situation; it was never occupied and was soon demolished.

Rushford Tower is the best-known and most convincing of the Dartmoor follies, giving the appearance of a small weather-worn make-believe castle, with a round tower, gothic doorway and lancet windows. It stands on private land at 702890 a mile to the north of Chagford.

An incongruous circular pillbox-shaped structure stands on a high point at **Scobitor Farm** (Widecombe, 725750). Built in the 19th century, it is reasonable to call it a folly, but its original purpose is not known. It does, however, command a good view of its surroundings, so putting a shelter in such a spot would have been a logical idea.

Folly at Scobitor

Castle Drogo (Drewsteignton, 722901), the last "castle" to be built in England, is in fact a pretentious granite dwelling-house, designed by Sir Edwin Lutyens for Mr.J.C.Drewe, and built in the years between 1911 and 1930. It is now in the care of the National Trust.

In an article in DM Winter 1989 Judy Chard mentions Filham near Ivybridge, just outside the National Park, where a ruined chapel of about 1400 was modified by the addition of a tower in 1800.

———— Odds and Ends ————

In 1854 James Perrott of Chagford, then known as the Dartmoor Guide, set up a small cairn at Cranmere Pool, placing therein a bottle for the visiting cards of those intrepid walkers who were successful in arriving at the spot. Cranmere Pool is situated on the "roof" of the northern moor, surrounded by peat bog (or "fen") and the sources of several of Dartmoor's main watercourses; the journey there was at that time an arduous undertaking from any direction. The bottle was succeeded by a series of more permanent receptacles, with the refinements of a visitors' book and rubber stamp. It became the custom for visitors to leave a postcard, addressed and stamped in the orthodox manner, to be collected and posted by a later visitor at a conventional GPO box.

More boxes were subsequently established at other sites, notably at Belstone Tors, Ducks Pool and Fur Tor. The Belstone box is said to have been put there in 1894, the normal practice being that anyone coming across it should not divulge its location. Ducks Pool is another boggy hollow, in the middle of the southern moor, where a box was established in 1938, with a plaque on a nearby rock in memory of William Crossing.

Arrival at Fur Tor can be regarded as a reasonable achievement. As with other boxes that followed, no discrete structure was erected there for the purpose, the box being hidden among the rocks.

By 1965 there were seven boxes out on the moor, the first signs of an acceleration being graphically portrayed when Tom Gant devised an illustrated record sheet in 1976, with spaces allocated for rubber stamp impressions from fifteen sites. There followed a meteoric rise in this activity, which continues unabated.

Cranmere Pool (Forest, 603858), a boggy hollow, is no longer difficult of access from the north, as the military road from Okehampton comes to within a mile, but it still presents something of a challenge from other directions, and retains its status as one of the principal focal points for the Dartmoor walker. It is thought that it was once a pool, its bank having been breached by tinning operations.

Ducks Pool (Forest, 625678) is the "Cranmere" of the southern moor. The metal box containing the rubber stamp and visitors' book is shown resting on the roof of its stone repository.

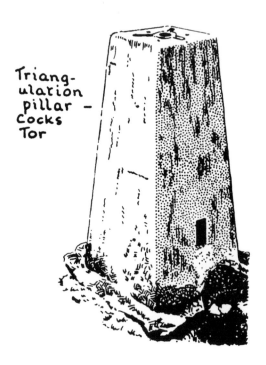

Triang-
ulation
pillar –
Cocks
Tor

Triangulation pillar. In the absence of suitably placed church towers or other prominent structures, OS "trig. points" (trigonometrical stations), in the form of concrete pillars, occur on several high spots, e.g. Bellever Tor, Cox Tor, Yes Tor, Ryder's Hill and Cosdon. Each is marked on the map by a dot in a triangle and a figure indicating its height (at ground level) above mean sea level. The natural desire that exists in most of us to make straight for the highest or most prominent feature in our vicinity has brought into existence such well-worn paths on the ramparts of Cranbrook Castle that arrangements were put in hand to replace the pillar there with an inconspicuous ground-level fixture. Most of the remaining pillars are now disused and have been offered for adoption.

Bibliography

Anthony, G.H. 1971. *The Tavistock, Launceston and Princetown Railways* The Oakwood Press.

Atkinson, M., **Burt,** R. and **Waite,** P. 1978. *The Dartmoor Mines.* University of Exeter.

Baring-Gould, S. 1907. *A Book of Dartmoor.* 2nd ed. Methuen.

Brewer, Dave. 1986. *A Field Guide to the Boundary Markers on and around Dartmoor.* Devon Books.

Burnard, Robert. 1890-94. *Dartmoor Pictorial Records.* Devon Books reprint, 1986.

Butler, Jeremy. 1991- . *Dartmoor Atlas of Antiquities.* 4 vols projected; 3 vols published. Devon Books.

Butler, Simon. 1986. *A Gentleman's Walking Tour of Dartmoor.* Devon Books reprint.

Byng, Brian. nd. *Dartmoor's Mysterious Megaliths.* Baron Jay, Plymouth.

Chudleigh, John. 2nd ed. 1893. *Devonshire Antiquities.* Facsimile reprint by John Pegg Publishing, 1987, under the title *An Exploration of Dartmoor's Antiquities 1892.*

Crossing, William. 1888. *Amid Devonia's Alps.* David & Charles reprint 1974.

- 1901. *One Hundred Years on Dartmoor.* David and Charles reprint, 1967.

- 1902. *The Ancient Stone Crosses of Dartmoor and its Borderland.* James G. Commin, Exeter.

- 1903. *Dartmoor Worker.* Peninsula Press reprint, 1992.

- 1905. *Gems in a Granite Setting .* Devon Books reprint, 1992.

- 1906. *Princetown - its Rise and Progress.* Quay Publications, 1989 - first reprint in book form.

- 1912. *Guide to Dartmoor.* Peninsula Press reprint, 1990.

Dartmoor Magazine, a quarterly publication first issued Winter 1985. Quay Publications, Brixham.

Dartmoor National Park Authority. 1979. *Building in the National Park.* Bovey Tracey.

Dartmoor Newsletter. Ed. Paul Rendell. Bi-monthly. Plymouth.

Dartmoor Preservation Association. 1983. *A Dartmoor Century, 1883-1983.*
- *The Dartmoor Bibliography* and supplements. Other publications including frequent Newsletters.

Devon Archaeological Society. Proceedings; Newsletters; *Devon Archaeology.* R.A.M. Museum, Exeter.

Devon County Council. Devon Sites and Monuments Register. Kept at County Hall, Exeter, and may be seen by appointment.

Devonshire Association for the Advancement of Science, Literature and Art. Annual Report and Transactions (TDA), and twice-yearly Newsletter. Exeter.

Dines, H.G. 1956. *The Metalliferous Mining Region of South-West England.* Mem. Geol. Survey. HMSO.

Durrance, E.M. and **Laming,** D.J.C. (Eds.) 1982. *The Geology of Devon.* University of Exeter.

Ewans, M.C. 1964. *The Haytor Granite Tramway and Stover Canal.* David and Charles.

Fleming, Andrew. 1988. *The Dartmoor Reaves.* Batsford.

Fox, Aileen. 1964. *South West England.* Thames and Hudson.

Gill, Crispin (Ed). 1970. *Dartmoor, a New Study.* David and Charles.

Gordon, Ruth St.Leger-. 1965. *The Witchcraft and Folklore of Dartmoor.* Hale.

Greeves, Tom. 1985. *The Archaeology of Dartmoor from the Air.* Devon Books/DNPA.

Grinsell, L.V. 1978. *Dartmoor Barrows.* ProcDAS No 36.

Hamilton-Leggett, Peter. 1992. *The Dartmoor Bibliography.* Devon Books in association with the DNPA.

Harris, Helen. 1968. *The Industrial Archaeology of Dartmoor.* David and Charles. Rev. 1972, 1986. 4th ed., comprehensively revised, Peninsula Press,1992.

Harvey, L.A. and **Gordon,** D.St.Leger-. 1953. *Dartmoor.* Collins' New Naturalist.

Hawkings, David J. 1987. *Water from the Moor.* Devon Books.

Hemery, Eric. 1983a. *High Dartmoor - Land and People.* Hale.

   - 1983b. *Walking the Dartmoor Railroads.* Rev. ed. 1991 Peninsula Press.

   - 1986a. *Walking Dartmoor's Ancient Tracks.* Hale.

   - 1986b. *Walking the Dartmoor Waterways.* Rev. ed. 1991 Peninsula Press.

Hoskins, W.G. (Ed). 1957. *Dartmoor.* (National Park Guide No 1) HMSO.

Ivimey-Cook, R.B. 1984. *Atlas of the Devon Flora.* Devonshire Association.

Kendall, H.G. 1968. *The Plymouth and Dartmoor Railway.* The Oakwood Press.

Kingdom, A.R. 1979. *The Princetown Branch.* The Oakwood Press.

le Messurier, Brian. 1965. *The Phillpotts Peat Passes of Northern Dartmoor: a Pioneer Survey.* TDA Vol 97.

   - 1979. *The Post-prehistoric Structures of Central North Dartmoor.* TDA Vol 111.

   - 1980. *Dartmoor Walks for Motorists.* Warne.

Linehan, Mrs.C.D. 1965. *Deserted Sites on Dartmoor.* TDA Vol 97.

Martin, E.W. 1958. *Dartmoor.* Hale.

Martin, W.Keble. 1965. *The Concise British Flora in Colour.* Ebury Press and Michael Joseph.

Masson Phillips, E.N. Numerous papers in TDA, particularly on wayside stones (crosses, boundary stones, guide stones, milestones). Stone crosses in Vols 69-72 (1937-40), 75 (1943), 86 (1954), 111 (1979), 116 (1984). Roadside stones in Vol 75 (1943).

Moore, Robert. 1969. *The Birds of Devon.* David and Charles.

Ordnance Survey. 1962. Map of Southern Britain in the Iron Age. Reprint 1967.

Page, J.L.W. 1889. *An Exploration of Dartmoor.* Seeley.

Pearce, Susan M. 1981. *The Archaeology of South West Britain.* Collins.

Perkins, J.W. 1972. *Geology Explained: Dartmoor and the Tamar Valley.* David and Charles.

Pettit, Paul. 1974. *Prehistoric Dartmoor.* David and Charles.

Pilkington, Francis. 1978. *Ashburton: The Dartmoor Town.* (P/p).

Prince, Elizabeth. 1987. *Dartmoor Seasons.* Devon Books/DNPA.

Robins, John. 1982, 1983, 1984. *Follow the Leat.* P/p.

   - 1988. *Rambling On.* John Pegg Publishing.

Robinson, R., **Griffiths,** D. and **Cosford,** J. 1990. The Corringdon Multiple Stone Rows: a Re-survey. ProcDAS No 48.

Rouse, G.D. 1972. *The New Forests of Dartmoor.* (Forestry Commission Guide). HMSO.

Rowe, Samuel. (Rev. ed. 1896). *A Perambulation of Dartmoor.* Devon Books reprint, 1985.

Sanderson, Robert. nd. *The Prison on the Moor.* Westway, Plymouth.

Simmons, I.G. (ed). 1964. *Dartmoor Essays.* Devonshire Association.

Sitters, H.P. (ed). 1988. *Tetrad Atlas of the Breeding Birds of Devon.* Devon Bird Watching and Preservation Society.

Smith, Vian. 1966. *Portrait of Dartmoor.* Hale.
Starkey, H.F. (Harry). 1980. *Exploring Dartmoor.* P/p.
  - 1981. *Exploring Dartmoor Again.* P/p.
  - 1983. *Dartmoor Crosses and Some Ancient Tracks.* 2nd ed. 1989. P/p.
  - 1984. *Odds and Ends from Dartmoor.* P/p.
  - 1986. *Dartmoor Then and Now.* P/p.
Tregonning, Lance. 1983. *Bovey Tracey an Ancient Town.* P/p.
Turner, J.R. 1984. *A Possible Henge at Teignhead.* ProcDAS No 42.
  -1990 *Ring Cairns, Stone Circles and Related Monuments on Dartmoor.* ProcDAS No 48.
Wade, E.A. 1982. *The Redlake Tramway.* Twelveheads Press.
Walmesley, Mary and Jessica. 1982. *The Old Men of the Moor.* Stockwell.
Walsh, P. and **Byng,** B.A. 1985. *Burrator - A Pictorial Record.* P/p.
Ward, S.D., **Jones,** A.D. and **Manton,** M. 1972. *The Vegetation of Dartmoor.* Field Studies Vol 3, No 4, 505-533.
Weir, John (ed). 1987. *Dartmoor National Park.* Countryside Commission Official Guide. Webb and Bower/Michael Joseph.
Woods, Stephen H. 1988. *Dartmoor Stone.* Devon Books/DNPA.
Worth, R.Hansford. Collected papers ed. **Spooner,** G.M. and **Russell,** F.S. 1953. under the title *Dartmoor.* David and Charles reprint 1967, entitled *Worth's Dartmoor.*

Note
P/p = published privately

Index